Copyright © 2020 by Leanne Maskell

All rights reserved. Disclaimer: the content of this book is for informational purposes only and is not intended to diagnose, treat, cure or prevent any condition. This book is not intended to be a substitute for consultation with a qualified medical professional or a direct expert, who you should consult regarding the suggestions and recommendations made in this book.

Anything that is expressed in this book is my own personal opinion and not intended to reflect in any way regarding any employers that I may have or had in the past. Although every effort has been made to ensure that the information in this book is accurate, no responsibility is assumed for errors, inaccuracies, omissions or any other inconsistencies.

This book is dedicated to everyone who has ever thought that there is 'something wrong with them', but who couldn't figure out what it was. Everyone who has been told that they're being 'dramatic', or that ADHD isn't real, or who has had to wait months or years to receive help. It is for the people who have felt so overwhelmed by the tsunami that is their own mind that they didn't know how they could go on any longer, but who have somehow kept fighting. For everyone who has felt like they're in an ocean that's filled with fish swimming one way, and you can only swim the other way. For all of the people who have felt like the 'odd one out', because they see the world differently.

I wrote this to provide an overview of my personal experiences in relation to ADHD, in the hope that it can help somebody else in a similar position. It's not here to convince you that you have ADHD and I'm no medical expert, just a person who has navigated this immensely difficult process and managed to finally live a stable, happy life with ADHD. This book is here as a gentle reminder that **you are not alone. You are worthy of existing in this world exactly as you are, and your pain is not your fault.**

Thank you to everyone who has helped me along the way, including my family, who have always tried their best with what they had available to them at the time. A special thank you to Rebecca Pearson, for being my inspiration, accountability buddy and best friend. Thank you for your constant support and accepting me unconditionally for who I am.

THE A TO Z OF ADHD

LEANNE MASKELL

Contents

A is for ADHD 5
B is for Burnout 15
C is for Confidence 23
D is for Diagnosis 32
E is for Exercise 45
F is for Finance 50
G is for Grounding 60
H is for High-functioning 70
I is for Interests 80
J is for Jobs 86
K is for Kindness 100
L is for Love 109
M is for Medication 118
N is for No 133
O is for Organisation 146
P is for Procrastination 160
Q is for Quitting 170
R is for Rejection 179
S is for Sleep 187
T is for Time Management 198
U is for Unite 206
V is for Vices 214
W is for Weaknesses 221
X is for X-rated 230
Y is for Your Body 243
Z is Zen 257

A

is for ADHD

Did you know?

- Attention Deficit Hyperactivity Disorder (ADHD) is a neurodevelopmental condition that is associated with high levels of impulsivity, hyperactivity and inattention. Though there are different subtypes, ADHD is now generally used as the official recognised medical term (instead of Attention Deficit Disorder), regardless of whether a person has symptoms of hyperactivity.

- Children and adults can both be diagnosed with ADHD. In 1990, only 40 children in the UK were on medical treatment for ADHD, which means many adults have not been treated or managed properly (LANCuk, 2016/2). Symptoms can appear differently at different ages.

- There are structural differences in the brain between those who have ADHD and those who do not (Cherney, 2019). Though there is no clear cause, it is said to be highly heritable, with a 75% genetic contribution of ADHD (Vanbuskirk, 2018).

ADHD stands for attention deficit hyperactivity disorder. There are different types of ADHD within this –the 'hyperactive and impulsive', the 'inattentive' type, or a combination of the two. The inattentive type is sometimes referred to as attention deficit disorder (ADD), but ADHD is the predominantly used medical term, as the subtypes are considered to fall under the same condition.

For this reason, you might not be diagnosed as a specific 'type' - I wasn't. There is no typical ADHD profile, despite the image of a hyper-active child that your mind may have automatically conjured up. I was the dreamy girl in the back of the class, staring out of the window, completely unable to listen and quite often falling asleep. I hated P.E but my knees often jiggled under the table, and was very quiet in social settings but my mind was constantly racing with thoughts.

However, there are common ADHD symptoms that might appear differently in different people who have ADHD (referred to as ADHD-ers):

- **Having a short attention span and being easily distracted**

    This basically summarises ADHD in one line - an intense difficulty in concentrating. The short attention span means that we may have 'monkey brains', jumping between thoughts like a monkey hopping from one tree branch to another without stopping. My brain often feels like a television with 15 channels playing at the same time, and the remote is nowhere to be seen. It can make things like listening very difficult!

- **Hyper-focus**

    In sharp contrast to the above point, ADHD-ers may have an ability to hyper-focus on something that they are interested in, focusing so much that they stop thinking about other things that might be important. For example, working on a project for the entire day without eating any meals. This can cause frustration as we *can* pay attention if it is something we're truly interested in - but if not, then it is incredibly difficult to motivate ourselves.

- **Carelessness and a lack of attention to detail**

Many ADHD-ers are 'big picture' thinkers. They may have brilliant ideas, but not be so great at executing them down to the minute details. I feel as though my brain works at a speed of 150%, which means that I can forego details in the rush of thinking fast.

- ❏ **Being unable to stick to tasks that are tedious or time-consuming**

    ADHD-ers might be very quick to say 'yes' to things, without checking the details, for example, thinking about whether they *actually* want to do something - the difficult bits included. We tend to not deal so well with repetitive, administrative tasks and are on a constant search for novel and exciting challenges. Doing something seemingly easy but a bit dull, such as washing clothes, might be incredibly difficult for a person with ADHD to wrap their heads around.

- ❏ **Disorganisation**

    Forgetting appointments, dates and possessions, losing things, being fairly messy – these are all traits of a classic ADHD-er. Prioritising can be difficult, as our brains search for the most appealing thing to be doing at that point in time, so things like cleaning may simply not get done. ADHD-ers typically struggle with deadlines and simple organisation, because the small things can seem so overwhelming.

- ❏ **Difficulty in completing projects**

    In line with the above, it can be very difficult to complete a project when your attention won't play ball! We might also struggle with instructions and following through on these, as we might lose concentration half-way through and completely forget what they were, especially if they're not written down.

- ❏ **Mental hyper-activity**

    My brain feels like it is constantly racing with thoughts and simply will not be quiet. One way of describing it is as though you are a 'human doing' instead of a 'human being' - it feels impossible to not be always thinking about something. This can translate to anxiety and an overwhelming amount of thoughts and worries going on at any one time, which can also manifest as talking very quickly or excessively.

- ❏ **Physical hyper-activity**

    The mental aspects can translate to physical restlessness, where a person with ADHD may feel unable to sit still, as though they are being driven by a motor that makes them want to get up and walk around or fidget. This is where we often think of the screaming, hyper children most commonly associated with ADHD. In adults, it might often be seen as insomnia.

- ❏ **Impatience**

    As our brains are moving so fast, ADHD-ers tend to be pretty impatient. This can result in interrupting others as they speak, having trouble waiting our turn or being impulsive, making decisions without fully thinking them out.

- ❏ **Risky behaviour**

    ADHD-ers may be prone to seeking out adrenaline in the form of risky decisions such as excessive spending, or self-medicate with alcohol or drugs. Our brains tend to be on the search for novel and exciting experiences, and we tend to get bored quickly.

- **Mood swings and low self-esteem**

    ADHD is exhausting. Having the constant noise of thoughts in your head and seeming to upset people despite trying your absolute hardest often results in mood swings, from inspired highs to terrible lows. It can feel incredibly lonely having ADHD and like nobody understands you. ADHD-ers often suffer from 'rejection sensitivity dysphoria' as seen in 'R is for Rejection'.

    As in 'W is for Weaknesses', ADHD can also bring amazing benefits, such as:

- **Creativity**

    ADHD-ers think outside of the box and tend to be extremely creative people, who excel at solving problems. Many of the world's leading thinkers have had ADHD, such as Richard Branson.

- **Energetic**

    ADHD results in a lot of pent up energy, which can lead to burnout, as in 'B is for Burnout', but can be an amazing resource to draw upon.

- **Brave**

    ADHD-ers tend to be fearless, in their decision making, risk taking and choices.

- **Authentic**

When you have ADHD, you are motivated by passion and purpose, and whilst it can be very hard to find that purpose, it means that whatever you do, you will do it authentically, searching for true happiness.

- ❑ **Kind-hearted and compassionate**

    ADHD-ers generally care about others a great deal, having experienced many difficulties themselves in life and being sensitive to this.

- ❑ **Multi-tasking**

    Due to having several thoughts going on at the same time, people who have ADHD often are able to multi-task very well.

- ❑ **Calm in a crisis**

    The adrenaline rush of a crisis can result in the ADHD brain being in a 'normal' mode, meaning we are great in an extremely stressful situation.

ADHD impacts the prefrontal cortex in our brains, which is responsible for thinking, thought analysis and regulating behaviour, essentially regulating our short and long term decision making. It helps us to focus thoughts, pay attention and concentrate. It's the part that explains why we don't eat chocolate ice-cream for breakfast, lunch and dinner every day, or why we do things that we might not particularly 'want' to do, like going to the gym on a cold morning before work. Essentially, our responsible, 'adult' part of our brain.

In ADHD-ers, the prefrontal cortex is unregulated. There are no traffic lights slowing us down as we make decisions, no stabilisers on our imaginary bicycles preventing us from losing concentration and falling off as we become distracted by anything and everything. I've heard it referred to as having a 'Ferrari brain with Chevy brakes'. The adult in the room preventing us from eating the ice cream for breakfast seems to have gone on holiday, which means we have to work much harder than other people in *not* doing the things we are inherently drawn towards, like scrolling through social media in the mornings or thinking about what to reply to someone as they are speaking. Doing things that aren't 'fun', like figuring out our bills, are much more difficult for us to do than for the average person.

Our judgment is also managed here, conceptualising how long it might take us to complete a task. Time management is typically affected by emotions here for ADHD-ers, who may feel more stressed at the thought of completing a task than they do able to actually complete it. This is where procrastination, well known to ADHD-ers, enters the room. Whereas a person who doesn't have ADHD may be able to force themselves to 'get on with things', an ADHD-er may have to lock themselves in a room with no distractions in order to find the same level of motivation.

Emotions are regulated through this prefrontal cortex, which can explain the rapid mood changes that ADHD-ers are often accustomed to. We can often feel emotions very intensely, as though it is the only thing we can focus on in any given moment, which can result in impulsivity. I think of this in a similar way to how teenagers are written off as being 'hormonal' when they are emotional - ADHD-ers can find it much more difficult to control their emotions than others.

One of the reasons I didn't see ADHD as 'real' before being diagnosed was because I, like so many others, just thought I was being lazy and stupid. This is a big part of what prevents people from getting help with ADHD and at the same time makes it even worse to live with, because we are not only suffering with the symptoms, but also maybe being beaten up for having it at all – whether that is by ourselves or others in our lives. Being diagnosed is a huge act of compassion towards yourself, as you realise that the struggles you have encountered along the way are likely **because of your ADHD. Not because you are stupid, lazy or weak - but because you are neurologically diverse to others.**

Assessing your ADHD

A good starting point is to understand how ADHD affects you overall and what your motivations are. As seen, ADHD-ers tend to struggle with things they inherently don't want to do and may devote too much attention to things they are interested in. By understanding what makes you 'tick', you can figure out how to hack your own brain to make those more tedious things a little bit easier!

1. Write down how ADHD has affected you so far in your life. Even if you haven't been diagnosed with it or aren't quite sure, try just writing down how you feel like it could have possibly affected you. Try to approach this with a compassionate and kind mind towards yourself, accepting that this is a neurological condition that completely validates any difficulties you may have encountered as a result.

2. Make a list of 5 activities that you enjoy doing, and 5 things that you do not. Try to identify any similar themes between each category - for example, are the things you enjoy all exercise-based, or do they revolve around helping other people? Does the other list

revolve around things that are repetitive or detail orientated?

3. From this, assess your top 3 values - the things that motivate you in life. This could be love, validation, money, career achievements and so on.

4. Looking at these lists, try to identify 3 strengths - tools that you might typically use in the activities or values that are important to you. If you're not sure, ask some friends what they think your top 3 strengths are, or find an online personality test. These could include kindness, compassion, honesty, creativity and so on.

5. Assess how much of your life you are currently living in line with your strengths, values and activities you enjoy. Are there ways that you can increase the time spent on doing the things you enjoy?

6. Now look at the list of activities that you do not enjoy doing, and try to figure out a way to make them align with your values. For example, if you're motivated by friendship, could you set up an 'accountability buddy' to check in on how much administrative tasks you've completed each week?

7. Make a plan of 3 specific goals you might have that are related to your ADHD, and how you can achieve these. For example, you might want to stop making impulsive decisions, so a corresponding action could be to seek out a therapist or write down your decisions at the end of each day. Give yourself a generous timeline!

is for burnout

Did you know?

- Adults are usually diagnosed with ADHD after a burnout. It has been suggested that people with ADHD have had to put 500% in throughout childhood and exams, and just assumed everyone had to work as hard as they did (Ross, 2016).

- There is research to suggest that career success could be compromised by having ADHD, and that there are clear weaknesses in the UK & internationally to address occupational difficulties (Adamou, M., Arif, M., Asherson, P. et al, 2013).

- Adolescent girls with ADHD were found to be significantly more likely to attempt suicide or injure themselves than those who do not have ADHD (American Psychological Association (APA), 2012).

Burnout is commonly seen in ADHD-ers as a result of exhaustion and trying to meet unrealistic expectations, often self-imposed! ADHD-ers tend to have a lot of excess energy, especially when starting something new, or when they are inspired, which can see them working at incredible rates, often as a result of the hyper-focus that can accompany ADHD.

This effort level is generally unsustainable in the long run. This can be frustrating and de-motivating for others as well as the ADHD-er in question, who can beat themselves up for not being able to maintain this unrealistic energy. Our brains are simply not designed to run at this level of concentration for very long, but it can feel like we should be able to, simply because we sometimes can. It can contribute to feeling as though ADHD isn't a 'real' neurodevelopmental condition, because we can concentrate if we 'put our minds to it' - unfortunately it's often the other way around!

Burnout can come in many different forms. Physically, it can leave a person utterly exhausted to the point of illness, as their bodies simply shut down in an effort to make them stop, such as experiencing panic attacks and migraines. Mentally, this could look like cancelling plans, spirals of guilt and self-hatred, quitting commitments, and being mentally depleted to the point of total exhaustion.

The core concept for ADHD-ers to bear in mind is that **YOU CANNOT DO IT ALL.** Despite feeling that you can achieve anything that you put your mind to in the outset, it is so important to remind yourself that you are a human being like everybody else.

Counteracting burnout requires us to slow down and consider the reasons behind these feelings.

The below factors can often contribute to the temptation to over-exert yourself:

1. Insecurity

It is quite ironic that ADHD-ers may often place themselves under serious pressure to perform because of insecurities inherent in being unable to perform fully in the past. Placing unrealistic expectations on ourselves will usually mean that we are unable to meet them, which can lead to a lack of trust and low self-esteem. We also tend to be more sensitive to rejection, often suffering from 'Rejection Sensitive Dysphoria' as discussed in the chapter 'R is for Rejection', having likely been told off as a child for being neurologically diverse. Finally, our tendency to make impulsive decisions, can often result in negative experiences or being unable to commit, which all leads to more pressure when we try the next time.

Whenever I feel insecure, my coping mechanism tends to be firing ahead with solutions and pushing myself to work harder than usual. The ironic thing is that this often causes problems in itself, as other people may not want my well-meaning advice, and they may not understand the extra level of effort being put in, which all can lead to further insecurity and a further determination to work harder - until I hit burnout!

To tackle insecurities, it is good to make a list of any potential triggers and identify areas of your life where this could be an issue and how you react. This will help ensure that you are acting from a confident, assured place instead of out of fear.

2. Boundaries

ADHD doesn't go particularly well with boundaries. These require you to stop and think, to look at the arbitrary, imaginary line drawn by society, usually upheld in our minds by the adult-type-regulators hanging out in the prefrontal cortex - unless you have ADHD. This can be really frustrating, because without this regulation we often simply don't process these boundaries – ADHD-ers tend to see emotion and reason, rather than an arbitrary, bureaucratic process that may not make sense. It is very hard for us to fit into boxes that seem utterly pointless, to do something without understanding the *reason* why – and believing in that reason.

The good thing about this is that we tend to live very authentic lives, but the big negative is that most of our society tends to be made up of bureaucratic processes. Think of it like building blocks holding up this imagined community we have –

whether that is the entire world, your workplace or your family. Your parents exert authority 'because they say so' – even if it doesn't make much sense to you. If you don't agree with it, then you can argue back and ultimately find yourself out of a family – which we will see more of in 'L is for Love'. Similar issues often arise in the workplace, which might be part of the reason that ADHD-ers may struggle with keeping jobs on a long-term basis.

Problems with boundaries are inherent in people pleasing, as we will see in 'N is for No'. It is often an inability to say no that results in us trying to do everything and please everybody – usually at the expense of ourselves. Boundaries are important, because they keep us from burning ourselves out.

3. Hyper-focus, impatience and unrealistic expectations

People who have ADHD may need to do everything *right now whilst they can* because they want to do everything this minute - we tend to have two references for assessing time, 'now' and 'not now'. The concept of waiting, of things taking place over a few months as opposed to a few weeks, is difficult to imagine. This can tie in with the insecurity aspect – of feeling that maybe you won't be there in a few months to be able to do it, so it needs to be done right now.

If we are on the high of an exciting new project, we might also be overly-optimistic in how much energy we think we may think we want to commit to this project at the start. It can be difficult to slow down the excited adrenaline and think about things in a long-term way, and to accurately assess our own capabilities. ADHD-ers may find themselves setting unrealistically short deadlines for work projects, for example, despite issues with time management being one of the main symptoms!

Ultimately, burnout comes from over-committing yourself to too many things. It stems from problems with pausing, thinking and assessing before acting.

   4. Self-fulfilling prophecy

Many people live by 'stories', such as not being good enough to do X, Y or Z, and it can sometimes be easier to fulfil this prophecy than take a risk in actually applying ourselves and seeing what happens. It may feel easier to steam roll ahead in a flurry of ideas and feel like you have some control over your situation, even if it involves sabotaging it, than to be vulnerable enough to admit you don't know everything, to ask for help and learn from others.

Ultimately, burn-out stems down to problems in trusting yourself and others.

Ways to deal with burnout

The best way to deal with the cycle of burnout itself is to plan ahead.

1. Firstly, notice when the cycle starts. Think about times in the past when you may have overcommitted yourself and burned out, then try to spot the thing that links them together, such as stress.
2. Once you have your triggers, try to see how your burnout cycle plays out. Do you say yes to too many invitations, or make sure you are the last one in the office each night? Do you start new hobbies? Try to find the warning signs. I can usually tell when I am burning out by over-committing to lots of plans at the

same time, for example. Write down the things you do when you find yourself on the burnout rollercoaster.

3. Now, identify the negative things that have happened when you have burned yourself out before. Do you feel like you have let people down, or have you become physically unwell? Have you quit projects or plans, or simply cut people off?

4. Think about the things you have done in the past and try to feel the emotions connected with those actions. Accept however you may feel – whether that is guilt, shame, embarrassment or anything else – and try to give yourself some love. Write down a little note of encouragement to yourself to find the positives, even if it is just being able to reach this point. Maybe you want to say an apology to your body or gently acknowledge that situations may have been different to how you felt in the emotion of the time. Remember that you have only ever done the best with the resources you had available to you at the time.

5. Identify how you have burned out before and how you have felt better afterwards. Write down the things that make you happy and feel relaxed, such as exercise or journaling - these are your coping strategies.

6. Write down the ways you can stop yourself becoming burned out in the future, such as saying no, giving yourself breaks, or leaving yourself at least one free evening per week to relax. Try to find a 'burnout buddy' and share this plan with them, so they can intervene if they spot some of the signs of you potentially burning yourself out - you can offer to do the same for them!

Your plan is there to help you spot the triggers of potential burnout and to act before it happens. Every person with ADHD is different and will have different ways of coping best with stress.

Ultimately, the main thing to work on is self-compassion and self-worth, and confidence in yourself, which we will see in the next chapter. It is only when you are kind to yourself that you can turn up *as you are* with a simple confidence in that whatever you produce at a healthy level will be great. It is the confidence in knowing that you have time and that you will make the right decisions for yourself in the future, that you do not have to do everything, and other people's happiness is their responsibility. That you can say no, put yourself first and still be accepted.

C is for confidence

Did you know?

- There is evidence to suggest that ADHD is associated with lower self-esteem in adulthood (Cook, J., Knight, E., Hume, I. et al, 2014).

- It has been suggested that for every 15 negative comments a child with ADHD receives, there is only 1 positive comment (Saline, 2019).

- It's estimated about 18.6% of adults are affected by both ADHD and depression (CHADD, 2019).

Confidence is an elusive concept for ADHD-ers. It comes in waves – from having inspired confidence in your own ideas, thinking creatively and fearlessly taking risks, to crashing down with perceived rejection, failures and insecurities. It can be quite complicated for people to understand how you can be so overly confident one moment, to being so crippled with insecurity the next that you cancel all of your plans.

Overall, I believe that most people who have ADHD suffer from low self-esteem on some level, no matter how confident or successful they seem on the outside.

This would primarily come from childhood. ADHD is developmental, so as part of the diagnosis process, our early years are considered to assess how we may have been impacted throughout our lives. Thinking differently makes you different, which is no fun as a child just wanting to fit in. It might mean that you are bullied for your enthusiasm, told off for interrupting, chastised for not being able to pay attention in class, or find it hard to make friends. It might mean that the things you really love as a child, you are made to feel bad at, and take this on to mean that *you* are bad. These childhood experiences form our fundamental beliefs about ourselves and how we interact with others in the world.

People with ADHD may also suffer with imposter syndrome. I never felt intelligent, because I learned differently to everybody else - and yet never felt like I could admit I had a problem because I was objectively 'successful' in the eyes of others. I didn't feel like I deserved my good exam marks, because I was unable to concentrate throughout the year during classes, instead teaching myself the entire subject the week before an exam. I felt like I had cheated somehow, by learning differently – my teachers even asked my classmates if I had cheated when I got straight A's, which didn't help!

ADHD does not fit neatly inside the lines of the society that we have prescribed ourselves, which we are first introduced to as children. Having a neurodivergent brain means the you think differently to others, however we have schools that dictate certain ways of behaving, measurements of success and boxes to fit into. Our society prizes exam results and having a good 'status' job over whether we enjoy it, meaning that many people may be living a life that is not authentic to them. Having ADHD can make it impossible to fit into the box, but it doesn't mean that you are the problem.

Building confidence and self-esteem is critical to thriving with ADHD. Having ADHD can feel at odds with being confident, but once you learn how to manage this and grow confidence yourself, it becomes your tool. The innate sources of energy, inspiration and creativity that come with ADHD means that you have powers that other people do not have. Being different is your superpower - this is what should give you confidence, knowing that you see the world in an unique way, and that you have a way of thinking that other people do not have.

If you judge a fish by its ability to ride a bicycle, the fish will spend its life thinking that it is stupid.

Accepting that you have ADHD is the first step to increasing your confidence. If you know what the problem is, you can solve it. My life changed when I was diagnosed with ADHD because I finally allowed myself to have compassion for myself and the pain that I had felt throughout my life at being different, lazy and stupid – for something that was always out of my control. It helped me see that there was a reason for being the way I was, and accepting that I have ADHD gave me the keys to unlock myself. I stopped trying to fit myself into a neurotypical box, and beating myself up for not being able to think like I was 'supposed' to, instead freeing myself to think in my own way.

Low self-esteem can affect us in many ways – whether that is how productive we are, how we look, how popular we are or anything else we may feel insecure about. The irony is that insecure people often react to this by over-compensating (see 'B is for Burnout'!) but you might recognise patterns of acting out against your insecurities in yourself.

True confidence comes from knowing that you are enough, exactly as you are. You do not need to change yourself to fit in. You do not need to apologise for being who you are, for how productive you are, or for taking up space in the world. Having ADHD is not a burden to the people around you. It is just part of who you are, and that is simply a human being.

One thing that taught me to be a little kinder to myself is to picture a baby. The baby is loved simply for existing – it does not have to do anything, or be anyone in particular, to be deemed worthy of love. It actually can cry all day and be a fairly big nuisance, yet it is still loved all the same.

Likewise, someone we love who is unwell. If you imagine a close family member on their deathbed, all you want in the world is for that person to become better. You do not require them to have a certain job, be earning a certain amount of money or have a specific number of friends to be worthy of your love. You just love them regardless of anything else. That is the love that people feel towards you – whether you want to acknowledge it or not.

The secret to feeling confident is to be compassionate to yourself. Don't set yourself up for failure. If you feel confident, you are guaranteed to do a better job than not. Just look around you at the people in power, who are seemingly so overly confident despite their ideas not really making much sense at all. Confidence is the secret to success.

I became confident by understanding myself and finding hacks to it. For example, I know that I can concentrate best in the morning, rather than later in the day, so I take full advantage of my job's flexible working hours and start at 8am.

Having ADHD can feel like a hinderance to being confident, because there is a lot to be aware of in terms of how it can impact you. However, if you refuse to apologise for who you are, you are already winning. Accepting yourself and all of the quirks that you come with is half of the battle. Acknowledging these quirks – for example, by reading this book – allows you to truly accept them as part of who you are, and to like yourself regardless of whether anybody else does.

This comes with realising how we talk about ourselves and the inner voice that is narrating our life. I didn't realise until a friend pointed out how horrible I was being to myself on a daily basis, always putting myself down and calling myself ugly. I would never dream of speaking like that to anybody else.

Nowadays I try to be very mindful of what I say about myself around anyone, but an excellent way to think of your own insecurity is to imagine that is flowing out to the people around you. Imagine a mother calling herself fat in front of her daughter – who only sees a strong, beautiful woman in front of her but inherits the fear of being 'fat'. Imagine calling yourself stupid around your friends, who are condemned by nature to feel similar, such as the scene in the movie Mean Girls, where the young women berate themselves in the mirror as a form of bonding.

If you turned up to a dinner party and declared that you 'feel so fat today so won't be eating dessert', the other people there would maybe feel some of the shame gremlins finding their way onto their dessert plates. It would be a perfectly acceptable thing to say, something that has even been praised in our society – but it is making yourself and others around you feel bad. Contrastingly, saying that you 'feel so beautiful today' may feel very difficult in comparison, ironically for fear of judgment. It is bizarre that we see someone as embracing themselves as 'arrogant', but unfortunately this is the world that many of us live in.

Capitalism feeds off us feeling bad about ourselves, thriving on *insecurities*. If all the women in the world woke up tomorrow and were happy with how they looked, billion-pound industries would come crashing down overnight. For example, the fashion industry. Nobody needs *another white t-shirt*. However, if you feel like buying this white t-shirt will make you look richer, thinner, more beautiful, then you might be convinced into spending £20 on it. If it is modelled by a child, someone who triggers all the right insecurities in you to make you subconsciously want to buy that t-shirt, you might do it.

Choose to beat the system and to be confident in yourself. I can say with total 'confidence' that literally nobody cares about what you are doing – they are all far too busy worrying about themselves. Notice how you feel about other people and remember that is probably how they feel about you. If you try something and fail, nobody would think worse of you for it – they would most likely just forget within a few days.

You are the only person who cares about what you do, at the end of the day. Your confidence ultimately only matters to you. You aren't going to reach your deathbed and care about the things that your acquaintances got up to in their twenties or all of the times you held yourself back. Perfection is an impossible glass ceiling, and our failures are what make up our successes, teaching us new things every time. By embracing yourself and being your own biggest supporter, regardless of how many times you fall down, you can live your life with confidence and happiness.

How to beat insecurity

1. Identify what negative opinions you might have about yourself and why you think they are a problem. If none spring to mind, think about what makes you feel really angry, then look behind that – why do you feel angry? Have a think about why you feel these insecurities and

where they come from. For example, feeling 'bad' at managing bills, and linking this back to struggling in maths classes at school.

2. Make a tailored plan to tackle these insecurities, working on one at a time. Firstly, write the opposite statement down and all of the proof to back it up, such as 'I am good at managing bills. Proof of this includes having certain bills in my name, the supply of which has never been cut off!'

3. Identify ways that you can target this insecurity in a practical way. This might involve looking at the problem itself and acknowledging areas where you could use some help. For example, 'asking a friend how they set up standing orders for bills to be paid automatically each month'.

4. Dedicate some time to putting your method into action, for example, scheduling an hour at the end of a month to go through your bills and ensure they are all in order.

5. Write yourself a positive statement about the insecurity, such as 'I am in full control of my finances', and stick this on your bathroom mirror for a week.

6. Return back to this exercise regularly, especially whenever you notice that you are feeling particularly insecure about something. Remember that everybody has insecurities and the trick to beating them is acknowledging that they are simply stories we are telling ourselves!

How to grow your confidence

1. Write down a list of 30 of your achievements so far in life, no matter how small – these can definitely include 'getting out of bed on cold days' and 'finishing school'!

2. Identify your top 5 strengths - you could do this by assessing yourself, asking other people, or doing an online personality quiz. Once you have your top 5, look at how much you are using your strengths on a daily basis. Try to think of ways you could increase this.

3. Think about how someone who loves you would describe you. What impact have you had in their life?

4. Appoint a 'confidence friend'. Ask them to call you out every time you speak badly of yourself and note it down. Write the opposite proof down for every negative statement you say.

5. Spot what makes you feel insecure – is it talking to a certain person, or scrolling on social media? Decide to limit this in your life and notice the difference, for example, by staying off social media for a day. Make a conscious effort to stop comparing yourself to other people.

D
is for diagnosis

Did you know?

- There is no biological test for ADHD, so the diagnosis is made on the basis of a full developmental and psychiatric history, observer reports and examination of the mental state by a qualified specialist. (National Collaborating Centre for Mental Health, 2009).

- The waiting list for an ADHD assessment in the UK can take up to 7 years in some areas (ADHD Action, 2018). Around a third of people are thought to have waited over 2 years before they are formally diagnosed (Born to Be ADHD, 2017).

- In July 2020, Freedom of Information Requests to NHS trusts found at least 21,000 adults on waiting lists for ADHD services (BBC, 2020).

Being diagnosed with ADHD can be a very overwhelming and complicated process. There are very long waiting lists in the UK for assessments under the NHS, and private psychiatrists can be extremely expensive. However, it is important to know that you have a **legal right to choose the specialist to whom your GP refers you to**.

If your doctor agrees that you might have ADHD and wishes to refer you to a specialist for assessment, you can ask to be referred to Psychiatry-UK[1] (or any other qualified provider). As they are based online, assessments can happen within weeks rather than months or years.

Being diagnosed is not only helpful for treatment purposes such as medication, but mainly because of how liberating it is

---

[1] https://psychiatry-uk.com/right-to-choose/

to accept that you may have a neurodevelopmental condition, instead of beating yourself up for things that are not within your control.

However, it can also be an emotional rollercoaster and is important to remember that ultimately, it is one person's assessment: you are still the same person either way. No one can 'tell you for sure' whether you have ADHD or not – it is a subjective opinion of the specialist, but even specialists might have different opinions.

ADHD symptoms can commonly overlap or co-exist with other conditions and be misdiagnosed. There is a general lack of awareness about ADHD and stigma attached to it, even amongst professionals, and with it manifesting differently in everybody, it can be extremely hard to diagnose.

My experience

After graduating from University, I was very overwhelmed with trying to figure out 'what to do with my life', repeatedly making erratic, impulsive and self-sabotaging decisions. I just thought that this was me being unable to cope with the 'real world' but became extremely depressed and anxious as a result.

A year later, my life was an utter mess. I had very toxic relationships, lost friends, was doing a job I hated and was generally very unhappy. Eventually I Googled how I was feeling and self-diagnosed myself with *everything* I found (except ADHD!). I was absolutely terrified and was convinced that I'd be sectioned into a mental health hospital if I told anybody what I was experiencing.

Eventually I hit what I thought was 'rock bottom' and went to see a counsellor, feeling the most intense amount of shame and fear. Then I was angry to be told that I was paying £70 for somebody just to listen to me, and she couldn't diagnose me with anything or even tell me what she thought!

I visited many different doctors over the course of the next year with my symptoms when things became unbearable. The doctors refused to acknowledge that I had any problems other than possible 'emotional issues', because I appeared extremely 'self-aware, intelligent and was not about to rob a bank'. Which was a relief to hear in the moment, but very worrying as I walked out knowing that something had been missed. It felt like I was making a fuss out of nothing, just going to the doctor for being lazy and stupid.

Part of why being diagnosed is so hard is because it takes so much bravery to even acknowledge that you need help and then to go to a doctor in the first place to ask for this. It can be even harder if the doctor is saying what you ultimately want to hear – that you're fine – and you need to essentially prove to them that they are wrong.

I became obsessed with researching different mental health conditions to try and fill in the doctor's mistakes, which later developed into suicidal ideation. This was really scary to experience, and eventually I visited a private psychiatrist to try and get help.

The session costed approximately £400 for one hour. I listed all of my problems and he stopped me to ask 'Do you have problems concentrating? Do you find that you interrupt people often, and cannot stick at anything for very long?'

The questions he asked were all very relevant to my problems and described my life, but I had never thought about things in that way before. Eventually he said, 'You have ADHD. Nothing else.' I burst out laughing and said, 'ADHD is fine! That's not a real problem!'

The psychiatrist said that ADHD could not be diagnosed in one session, though I clearly had it, and very badly so. I was told to return for another £400 session, where he would assess the impacts on my life up to that point. However, I didn't return for an entire year because I spontaneously moved abroad whilst on holiday the next week. This is another hurdle for people with ADHD in being diagnosed – we might not have stable enough lives to even have GPs, let alone live in the same place whilst waiting months or years for an assessment.

Ironically, the year that I lived abroad whilst knowing I had ADHD helped me treat it somewhat naturally during that time, which is why this book is valuable. I know that the symptoms can be managed without medication, to an extent. I gave up alcohol completely, stopped eating sugar and became vegetarian. I became heavily into yoga and meditation. I watched my life change as I managed to slow down my thoughts and concentrate my efforts on managing my symptoms. I started to write a book and watched my self-esteem grow over the months that I lived there, as I began to treat myself with more compassion than ever before. This didn't mean that I no longer suffered from impulsive decisions, emotional instability and difficulties in relationships, however.

Fortunately, I returned to the UK and to the psychiatrist, knowing that I ultimately needed professional help. Although I felt embarrassed for not being able to deal with it by myself, I finally believed that ADHD was most definitely real.

On this second session, I was asked another long list of questions, and was given two forms to have my family or friends fill out who had known me since childhood. This part of the process can be upsetting, in acknowledging that you have may have been struggling until that point without being able to get help. Other people may also remember things differently to how you experienced them!

After I provided the forms, the psychiatrist prescribed me with medication, which was life changing in helping me to manage my symptoms, as discussed further in 'M is for Medication'. I was shocked to learn, however, that I would have to pay £300 per month to have this prescription **for the rest of my life**.

I asked whether there were any other options such as transferring to the NHS, which the psychiatrist advised against because of the need to be re-diagnosed (wasting the money I've already spent) and potential gaps in treatment. It was overwhelming to try and understand whether I actually even had ADHD or was being exploited financially, to navigate the side-effects of the medication and to try and figure out where I would find that much money! It felt like a tax on my mental health.

After a couple of months, I told the psychiatrist that I could not continue and wanted him to write a letter to my GP anyway. It seemed better in the long run to wait for another assessment on the NHS than to be locked into paying so much money. However, I was shocked to learn from my GP that they **could continue prescribing me medication perfectly fine from this diagnosis!** I was re-diagnosed on the NHS a few months later through a similar substantive process, but nothing changed in practice. Since then, I have been much better in having a collaborative and transparent approach to treatment with my GP.

This experience is largely the reason for this book, because someone shouldn't have to go through this confusing process in order to receive the help that they are entitled to.

What you might experience

Even just thinking about whether you may have ADHD, let alone being assessed and diagnosed with it, can be extremely overwhelming. Some feelings you might experience include:

Excitement

Learning about ADHD is exciting, as you can finally piece together your experiences in life. No, you're not weird! You are just neurodiverse! You might become hyper-focused on ADHD and talk to others a lot about it, expecting them to share your elation and relief.

As people with ADHD often attract others with similar personalities (we don't mind each other interrupting!), you might also be tempted to 'diagnose' others. Remember that you cannot diagnose anyone and are (probably!) not a medical professional qualified in making such assessments, so try to resist telling someone that they might have ADHD! If someone asks you whether you think they have it, advise them to speak to their doctor.

Though it is exciting, try to not attach too much of your identity to ADHD: you're still the same person, you can just have a bit more compassion for yourself now! It's also good to be careful about being selective in who you speak to about it, such as only those who know you well and who you trust.

Loneliness / sadness

This process can bring a lot of memories up from throughout your life where you have felt misunderstood or struggled because of your ADHD. You may also be able to understand the impact it has had on your relationships and feel isolated, overwhelmed and scared.

The requirement for input from your family and friends into the assessment process can be confronting, especially if you don't have strong lifelong relationships with others, possibly due to having ADHD! Others may also react uncertainly, as they can remember your experiences differently, especially if you were able to hide your struggles.

ADHD also comes with a lot of stigma, and it can feel very lonely if the people around you do not 'believe' in it. If this is the case, I advise reaching out to support groups such as ADHD Unlocked [2] to connect with others having similar experiences. It helps to have at least one person in your life to support you throughout this process, so please do try to find someone to talk to about what you are experiencing.

Being diagnosed with a neurodevelopmental condition does force you to realise that you are different from others, but you are not alone in this.

Fear

Thinking about ADHD can be scary, especially if you're not used to thinking about your 'mental health' and life experiences. Trying to figure out medical services and talking about your feelings to medical professionals can be very scary, but I promise it is worth it!

When I was too scared to tell anybody how bad things were, it stopped me from being able to get help. You are not alone in what you are experiencing and being diagnosed with ADHD

---

[2] https://members.adhdunlocked.co.uk/~access/a1c91f/

(or anything else!) does not change who you are. All it does is allow you to understand yourself better and receive treatment for any difficulties you are experiencing, if you need it. That treatment won't change who you are either: it will just (hopefully!) make your life easier. It's also much better to know about ADHD if you have it, than not to know and be suffering!

Remember that if you don't agree with the assessment of one specialist, you have options, and I would advise seeking other opinions until you find one you honestly agree with. The private psychiatrist put me on medication that was too high and caused me to have panic attacks, prescribing me anti-anxiety medication when I complained. Now I take a lower dose that I feel comfortable with, under the guidance of my GP. Ultimately, the only person you can trust to fully understand your own experiences is you.

Anger

Anger is normal, especially when realising that you have been struggling for a long time with something that was never within your control. The diagnosis process can also be so complicated that it is natural to feel angry at how difficult it might have been to get help throughout your life, including why others didn't pick up on it.

It helps to remember that everybody is just doing the best they can with what they have available to them. As ADHD is still such a relatively new concept that we are still learning so much about, I can understand why it wasn't picked up on earlier. For example, my parents took me to the doctors because I seemed unable to listen and concentrate as child, who said this was due to a build-up of earwax.

Happiness

Overall, you will hopefully reach a point where you feel happy, peaceful and a sense of self-acceptance in terms of whether you have ADHD or not.

As in 'W is for Weaknesses', ADHD comes with many brilliant aspects, such as compassion, creativity and fun. If you are diagnosed, your doctor should have a 'structured discussion' with you about how ADHD can affect your life. (National Institute for Health and Care Excellence, 2019). Treatment is generally holistic, so may include talking therapy, medication, or lifestyle changes such as exercise, and the overall point of this is for you to be happy and healthy.

Being diagnosed with ADHD was by far the best thing to ever happen to me, as I was able to finally take control of my life and live it how I wanted to, instead of trying to survive in a maelstrom of daily chaos.

How to get an ADHD assessment in the UK as an adult

- ❑ If you think that you may have ADHD and would like an assessment, fill in an accredited online symptom checklist[3], and take this to your GP. Be prepared to explain your symptoms honestly and why you think you have ADHD.

- ❑ If your GP agrees that you may have ADHD, they can refer you to a specialist for assessment. Ask your GP

---

[3] https://add.org/wp-content/uploads/2015/03/adhd-questionnaire-ASRS111.pdf

about typical waiting times and if you'd like to, ask to be referred to Psychiatry-UK[4], exercising your 'right to choose' under the NHS Constitution [5] (if based in England).

- ❏ Depending on your specific situation, you might wish to visit a private psychiatrist for an appointment. If you can, tell your GP about your plans and ask them whether they will be able to accept the referral from a private psychiatrist. They may be able to recommend one to you and write a letter of support. Look at different options and price ranges!

- ❏ Ask a couple of people that you trust to support you in this process, including accompanying you to any appointments or providing background information if required.

- ❏ When you visit the psychiatrist for an assessment, make sure that you are well prepared. Try to find any school reports that you may have and present a full picture of how ADHD may have impacted you throughout your life.

- ❏ If you are diagnosed privately, ask to be referred back to the NHS once you have been diagnosed, and for a copy of your diagnosis and any prescriptions that you may be given. If your assessment is on the NHS, your GP might be provided with the results directly, and should update you accordingly.

---

[4] Follow the instructions here if relevant: https://psychiatry-uk.com/right-to-choose/
[5] NHS Gateway Publication number 07661, "Choice in Mental Health Care", updated in February 2018

❑ Ask your GP to refer you to a therapist for support throughout this process, or consider finding your own if this is not possible, preferably one with experience in ADHD.

It may be that you are unable to be diagnosed with ADHD for one reason or another, and it might not be necessary if you have lived your life until now with relatively few problems. ADHD-ers tend to be very resourceful and develop amazing coping mechanisms throughout their life. Although it can be helpful to have the confirmation from a medical professional, it's not always necessary unless you are looking to gain something specific from this diagnosis.

If this is the case, I would recommend just remaining open to the possibility that you may have some aspects of ADHD and taking what you need from this book. It is difficult - but try not to overthink it!

There are several lifestyle changes as set out in this book that you can make to treat symptoms that do not require you to be diagnosed, as in 'M is for Medication'.

Above all, remember that having or not having ADHD, or any other mental health condition, does **not** mean that 'there is something wrong with you'. It is simply just part of who you are, just like your height or eye colour.

These conditions are ultimately thought up by humans and given to us as labels. We are all human beings with a huge range of emotions and brain activity. There is so much we have yet to learn about ADHD and being diagnosed with it simply allows you to know yourself better and **receive the help that you deserve.** It does not make you weak – it makes you strong.

If this chapter has made you feel emotional at the difficulties in receiving help that someone in this position may experience, please talk about it as much as you can. Raise awareness, write to your local MP, speak to your GP, or people that you know.

If you have someone with ADHD in your life and are looking for information on how to support them throughout this process, please try to remember to just accept them as they are and be there for them unconditionally. It's helpful if you can give your advice when asked for it but remember that the person might be feeling very overwhelmed, and extra-sensitive to your opinions about their experiences. Being reminded that we are loved regardless of having ADHD or not is extremely helpful.

is for exercise

Did you know?

- Studies have shown that regular physical activity can decrease the severity of ADHD symptoms and improve cognitive functioning (Pediatrics, 2019).

- Moderate to intense exercise has been found to provoke changes in many of the same neurochemicals and brain structures as popular prescription ADHD medications (Michael Lara, MD , 2012).

- Boys have been found to respond better to rigorous exercise, and girls to moderate exercise in managing ADHD symptoms (Michael Lara, MD , 2012).

ADHD is often associated with a dysfunction of a neurotransmitter in our brain called dopamine. Exercise encourages the production of dopamine, norepinephrine and serotonin in the brain and has been argued to have the same effect on the brain as the stimulant methylphenidate (Ritalin) (Stewart, 2013). Essentially, exercise can do the same thing for the brain as ADHD medication does – at least for a short period of time.

Exercise produces endorphins, making us feel happy, and allows us to burn off our excess energy – which ADHD-ers have a lot of! It calms us down, clears our minds and can act similarly to meditation, by making us focus on one activity for a while and 'being' in our bodies. I find that the television in my brain is muted when I am in an intense exercise class, for example, as all of my thoughts are focused on trying to stay conscious!

It can also allow us to build a structure and routine, which is extremely helpful for managing ADHD symptoms. This is where exercise ties into self-discipline and self-motivation, which is something that ADHD-ers can find themselves struggling with.

The key to understanding ADHD in general is to find things that you enjoy – your purpose. ADHD-ers are motivated by purpose, reason and *wanting to do something.* So if you want to motivate yourself to do anything at all, try to make it as easy and fun as possible for you to do. More generally speaking this might involve assessing what you value in life - for example, having a community. You can then try to apply these values to the things you don't want to do, such as finding a local running group and making new friends.

Martial arts has been linked with positive effects on ADHD symptoms (Michael Lara, MD , 2012), possibly because it incorporates a range of different brain activity including control, balance, timing and concentration. Any challenging complex physical activities could have similar benefits, such as ballet, ice skating, gymnastics, dance and mountain biking than aerobic exercise alone.

It's also good to know what you *don't* value or enjoy, so that you can work this into your motivation plan. I have previously spent an eye-watering amount of money on expensive gym memberships before going once and never going again. I have finally accepted that I am simply not a person who likes working out on a treadmill and become extremely bored trying to make myself exercise in these environments.

So, I found ways to make it as easy and enjoyable as possible for me. This means finding gyms as close as possible to my house or work and novel exercise styles that I enjoy, such as hot yoga or trapeze classes. The internet provides an opportunity to try out almost any exercise we like from the comfort of our own homes – figure out what that is for you!

Rewards can also help, for example, by purchasing a slightly more expensive one month membership rather than a six month membership, and telling yourself that you will join if you go a certain number of times in that month. This also helps me not to commit myself or to set expectations that I won't meet. Having exercise buddies or joining a team can also be helpful, in terms of being held accountable to showing up.

If I am working out early in the morning, then I sometimes will go to sleep in my gym clothes. This means all I have to do is get out of bed and out the door. Counting down from a certain number can help with the literal force you need to push yourself out of bed. I usually count down from 10 and find myself doing the act without thinking about it - as long as distractions such as my phone aren't in my way!

Exercise and figuring out your 'why'

1. Write down a list of the things that you enjoy doing physically – even if it is just lying down or going for a walk. Other ideas could include dancing, football, netball, running, yoga, weights – anything at all, even if it isn't a typical sport (I am particularly passionate about silent discos in the morning)!

2. Write down what has stopped you in the past from exercising – what your blocks are. Do you hate the fashion-show-esque pressure of the gym? The travel involved in getting to the gym? Being cold, or being too hot? The alcohol required for busting your best dance

moves in the club? Or is it too expensive? What does the voice in your head say when you don't want to get up to go to the gym?

Identify your top block.

3. Compare the two lists and try to identify an exercise that fits into both of these. For example, if you enjoy football but hate being cold, could this be indoor football? If you enjoy running but hate the gym, could you start jogging outside? If you enjoy yoga but can't afford a membership, can you find free classes on Youtube to do in your bedroom? Be imaginative!

4. Do some research. Identify *one* new exercise that is realistic, achievable and affordable. This might mean in terms of location, fitness level, commitment required or anything else that you might think of.

5. Make a plan. The best way to try new things out is to refer back to 'C is for Confidence', and to just go for it! Go along to a session, sign up online, be brave enough to go alone. Literally nobody is looking at you and everyone is far too busy worrying about themselves. Make yourself a commitment to do it for a specific period of time (even just once!), with a reward at the end. Try to be as specific as possible and make it as easy as possible for you to stick to – start small.

It is important to remember not to overdo it. When we find something we really enjoy, we have a tendency to go all in and inevitably, burn out. One aspect of this is financial, as we will see in the next chapter – starting and stopping new hobbies can be pretty expensive!

is for finance

Did you know?

- Studies have shown that individuals with more severe ADHD symptoms during childhood have more difficulty paying bills and are more likely to be in debt as adults, have less savings and more likely to delay buying necessities (Liao, 2020). It was suggested that medication can mitigate these problems.

- Adults with ADHD are far more likely than those without to engage in risky financial behaviour, such as taking out expensive loans or impulsive purchases without thinking the implications through fully (Meijer, 2019).

- Saving money can be very hard for people with ADHD (Meijer, 2019), as it is difficult to plan for the future or think about things in the long-term, as in 'T is for Time Management'.

Having ADHD can be expensive. The combination of acting on impulsive thoughts, inattention to detail and lust for adrenaline can result in many expensive decisions that can keep you looped into an addictive cycle – feeling guilty for purchases and buying yourself more to feel better. This isn't even to mention the fact that people who have ADHD can struggle with holding down jobs and a stable income.

If your ADHD amounts to a disability, there may be government support available to you. This could include things such as Access to Work, as in 'J is for Jobs', which can provide funding for measures that can help you stay in employment, such as a job coach or special equipment. There are a range of potential benefits that can help, so definitely do your research in understanding where and how you can be supported – the UK Government lists these online.[6]

Saving arguably doesn't come naturally to any of us, let alone people who have ADHD. Things like tax, numbers and budgeting can seem complicated and detail orientated – we tend to live in the now, which can make life difficult in the future. For example, if you are self-employed, then you will need to put aside a portion of your income each month to save for a tax payment at the end of the year. If you have a rental agreement, you may need to make sure that you have enough income each month to be able to afford the rent. If you have an overdraft, this can often seem like free money - especially if you have difficulties keeping up with the logistics (such as remembering all of the different passwords – see 'O is for Organisation') to keep track of what you are spending.

Luckily, there are many different ways of making managing our finances easier these days. There are apps such as Monzo which you can put a certain amount of money onto each month and 'lock away' money in pots which cannot be accessed. Monzo also notifies you every time you spend money, which is a great reminder of how much you are spending. As we become more of a cashless society with online spending, it has become easier than ever to spend money without realising.

Online banking is a very helpful way to keep track of your outgoing payments, which are helpful to review regularly and properly appreciate how you are spending your money. You should also be able to choose not to have an overdraft option, which prevents the risk of falling into debt. It's worth speaking to any service providers that you make regular

---

[6] https://www.gov.uk/financial-help-disabled.

payments to and asking whether you can set similar 'spending limits' – I have one with my phone provider which means I never need to worry about accidentally racking up huge bills!

When it comes to finance, everyone is in a different financial situation and will manage their money differently. Some people have unhealthy habits in relation to online shopping, others to gambling, or signing up to new memberships that can easily be forgotten about. It's helpful to identify any patterns of problems you might be encountering. Unfortunately, the world we live in has made it easier than ever for us to fritter away money mindlessly. The 'subscription-era' is not well-suited to the impulsive nature of ADHD, as free trials and seemingly small purchases can quickly add up to large chunks of money.

Subscriptions are designed to make it hard to quit. When you sign up to a free trial, you will often have to cancel within a certain period otherwise the subscription will auto-renew. The cancelling process can be quite bureaucratic and difficult, having to go onto different pages, remember various passwords, and speak to a range of people. It requires sustained mental effort on something that is fairly boring and can seem pointless when it is a 'small' cost.

If you are anything like me, you will also have signed up to a fair few of these free trials with different email addresses and passwords. Trying to figure out all of the accounts and passwords can literally feel like banging your head against a brick wall – but it is worth it.

Some golden rules for people who suffer with ADHD are:

1. AVOID SUBSCRIPTIONS AND FREE TRIALS. If you *must* then write down your accounts and passwords in

a designated (hidden!) journal – see 'O is for Organisation' for more. Set yourself reminders of when these renew on your phone a few days in advance and make sure you cancel them, if you want to.

2. Avoid websites that make it very easy to purchase things. I noticed a thought pattern developing in me where I would literally wake up and think of things that I needed to buy, buy them and forget. I loved the adrenaline high of coming home to presents I forgot that I'd ordered – but not the huge amount of money it involves. This includes websites that sell everything you could possibly think of, which result in seconds between having the thought and purchase. Block them off your phone if you have to - I do!

3. AVOID DEBT! If you are in debt, consider options such as talking to charities that can support you or organisations such as Debtors Anonymous, and make a plan to get out of it as soon as you can. Try to avoid any forms of debt, even if it doesn't seem like debt in the form of taking out a loan - such as 'late payment' options or buying products on 'credit' and signing up to contracts where you pay them back over the long term. These can quickly spiral out of control and it's very difficult to keep track of the different interest rates that you might be being charged. =

4. Try to avoid free shipping. It might not seem to make sense in intentionally setting yourself a higher cost to purchase something, but that one thought process of 'oh this shipping will cost me £3.50. Do I *really* need this?' is important. It's essentially trying to make as

many of these types of 'do I need it?' thoughts as possible. For me, accounts with free next day shipping tend to be the worst for my impulsive buys, so I avoid signing up to 'cheap' monthly memberships which offer these.

5. Keep the bulk of your money in one or two savings account that are difficult to access, with standing monthly payments arranged to come from these, such as bills. Designate one bank account for 'spending', where you can pay yourself a budget each month. Try to avoid any overdraft options and if possible, for you to be notified every time you spend money.

6. Try to avoid having your bank card enabled for spending on your phone. The idea is to make it as hard as possible for you to spend money – so you have to actually get your card out of your pocket before spending money on something you might not need. Cash could also be a good option (though I tend to spend all of it whenever I have some!) – know yourself and what works best for you in terms of delaying the time between 'I want to buy that' and actually buying it.

7. Avoid buying things that have free returns. We want to reduce the bureaucracy involved *after* a purchase but increase the bureaucracy *before* one. Personally, I cannot deal with going to the post office and the processes involved to return a purchase – I'd rather just keep it.

8. Avoid spending money on apps. These are designed to be easy to purchase and difficult to cancel – and it can be hard to keep track of what you do and do not use.

Make a rule to yourself to never sign up to any trials or apps.

9. Notice if other people expect you to spend money on them. As ADHD-ers tend to detest details and be susceptible to people pleasing, others around you may be used to you picking up the dinner bill when it is too much faff to split it individually, or to follow up afterwards to ask to be repaid. Make a conscious effort to not spend money on anybody but yourself for a while and to avoid taking the role of 'pay me back later'.

10. Be mindful about your spending. By keeping a spending diary and physically asking yourself before each purchase if something is absolutely necessary, you can keep track of how you spend your own money.

11. Keep a 'virtual shop' in a diary. When you want to buy something, write it down in a notebook. This will satisfy the part of your brain that wants to feel like it's 'acted' upon the thought, and if you can, dedicate a specific 'buying' time of the week or month to look at the notebook and potentially act upon it. I often find that I don't actually want the things even a day later!

How to make a budgeting plan

1. Do a mindful financial self-assessment

Print out your most recent bank statement. Go through it and write out every recent purchase and whether it was necessary or not, and try to identify the thinking behind it. Notice if it was useful looking back, and whether you regret purchasing it.

Ideally for a week, but even for one day, write down every time you want to purchase something and the reasons behind it. Try to catch yourself and notice *why* you want to buy something and whether it is really necessary.

2. Identify your income and necessary expenses each month.

This does not include Netflix – it is the outgoing costs that are necessary for your survival. Such as electricity, water, rent and groceries - the bare minimum. Observe these two total figures and look at what you have when you subtract the necessary costs from your income. This is your spending money.

3. Make a clean start

Identify any 'unnecessary' subscriptions that come out of your account each month and cancel them. See if you can live without them for a month. Make yourself commit to sitting for 25 minutes at a time and cancelling your subscriptions. If you find that you need them after a month, you can return, but give yourself a break and make a fresh start from zero. This counts even for yearly subscriptions, make the effort of cancelling all of them in one go.

4. Choose how you want to spend and save your money

It's helpful to use an app like Monzo where you can put a specific amount of spending money each month. There are ways that you can put half of the money in a pot that is unlocked half way through the month, or saving pots that you can only access on certain dates. Simplify your spending and saving to the bare minimum of bank accounts – a saving and spending account.

If you want to start saving money, start small. Even just £10 per month can make a difference – that is £120 per year, the equivalent of two coffees a month. Choose a small amount to save each month and stick to it. You can always increase it in the future, but don't start with trying to save hundreds and failing straight away. Learn the art of slow saving.

With your remaining money, choose what you want to do with it. Do you want to split it into two sections? Do you tend to spend a lot at the start of the month? What are your weaknesses? Make a plan of how you want to spend your money and on what – this could be experiences, a holiday or clothes – but whatever it is, make sure that you actively choose it.

5. Make a blockage plan

Your bank account will show your weaknesses. If there is something you want to stop spending money on, such as clothes from a particular online shop, or eating out, make a plan to focus on making this as hard as possible for yourself. This could involve blocking certain websites from your browser, deleting certain apps from your phone, limiting yourself to one restaurant meal per week, taking lunch into work with you – whatever it is, you know how to target it. Start small and build up slowly.

For example, if you buy lunch every single day of the week, resolve to take in a lunch for just one day. Knowing that you *can* do it if you want to is the first step to breaking these habits.

6. Check in at the end of the week

Set yourself a reminder on your phone to check your bank account at a time when you know you will have 10 minutes to look at it. Review your spending each week and notice any differences in your finances overall. Remember not to beat yourself up if you still have an impulsive spend, but just to acknowledge it. If you can, find an accountability buddy to go through your spending each weekend with - me and my best friend go through our total weekly spending every Saturday on the phone!

G

is for grounding

Did you know?

- It is estimated that between 7-40% of people in the criminal justice system may have ADHD, though in many cases this may not be formally recognised. A Swedish study found that people with ADHD are more likely to commit crimes (37% of men and 15% of women) than those without it (9% of men and 2% of women). Medication was proven to reduce this. (Karolinska Institutet, 2012).

- Adults with ADHD are 9 times more likely to end up in prison than those of a similar age and background who do not have ADHD. They also experience more financial instability and are more likely to have been fired from a job (Born to Be ADHD, 2017).

- Mindfulness meditation has been found to be effective in treating adults with ADHD, following a study in 2017 (Mitchell JT, McIntyre EM, English JS, et al., 2017). This has been equated with focusing one's attention on the present moment with 'purpose', then approaching that moment with open-mindedness.

ADHD-ers tend to be filled with ideas and move very quickly through life, which is a brilliant thing, but can also mean being almost too busy to actually be present and 'live' fully, or to think things through. Grounding yourself is essential to thriving with ADHD, providing a structure and routine to your life in which you can flourish - and controlling the impulsivity aspect of your ADHD.

It can be very difficult to ground yourself and to enforce some stability into your life when everything is so fast-moving and exhilarating. I used to dread the idea of a routine and knowing what I will be doing each day, thinking this would make for a predictable, boring life. However, this predictability is what allows us to feel secure enough to live our lives to the fullest. Having a routine gives us the structure in which we can grow, something to tether us to the earth, the thing that we can always return to.

Anxiety is commonly linked to ADHD. I believe this is a direct effect of being crippled with worry over seemingly easy tasks, such as administration and cleaning, which can feel very overwhelming combined with beating ourselves up for not being able to do them. In contrast, daring activities such as bungee jumping or moving to a new country can seem comparatively easy – we tend to be good in a crisis because of the adrenaline that stimulates our brains. Contrastingly, the small things that most people are able to do on autopilot can easily all pile up into one insurmountable chore-mountain of stress.

This is where grounding steps in. Having a routine allows you to train yourself to do these small tasks on autopilot mode. It is training yourself to do these small tasks easily, bringing yourself into the moment and understanding that the world will not spin out of control if you sit still. It allows you to know what to expect and to stop worrying about it all – the framework for your life is in place.

There are a variety of ways that you can ground yourself, and each person will be different in what helps them feel secure and stable. If none of the below apply, try thinking of your own grounding method – which could be anything at all, from a pet, to a sport, to religion.

Finding a routine

A routine is a sequence of actions regularly followed. It can be anything from drinking the same drink in the morning to spending an hour on your phone when you wake up. The point of this is to find the *right* routine for you, that helps you feel grounded and secure. Something that does not change, no matter where you are in the world or what is happening in your life. Think of having a routine like the scaffolding around you as a human being, the structure that keeps you steady and upright.

There are many different ways of finding a healthy routine, which will depend on the person. Above all, it needs to be **realistically achievable and sustainable**. A morning routine is a good place to start, with an additional evening routine as an ideal end goal.

Think about what your morning currently looks like. How long do you have between waking up and leaving the house? Do you feel stressed out in the mornings, or forget things? What could you add in to make things a little more peaceful for yourself?

Ideas for a morning routine could include:

- ❑ Waking up half an hour earlier
- ❑ Meditating
- ❑ Drinking a glass of water or hot drink as soon as you wake up
- ❑ Waking up at the same time every day
- ❑ Doing exercise, such as yoga or going for a run

- ❑ Writing in a journal
- ❑ Having the same breakfast every day
- ❑ Making your bed

I would advise trying to incorporate a morning routine that you do *before* looking at your phone - where it is very easy to fall into a scrolling vortex! The problem with our phone is that it tends to rule us, rather than the other way around, as it has been designed by experts to be as addictive as possible. Even if we go on to look at one thing, our attention tends to become sidetracked into things we may not have intended to start out day with, such as negative news or social media.

Try to limit your phone usage in the mornings in particular – remember that how you start your day sets the tone for the rest of it. One idea to limit phone usage in the mornings is to charge it in a different room to the one you sleep in – and invest in an alarm clock!

As we will see in 'O is for Organisation', there are also things that you can incorporate into your morning routine that will make your life easier for the rest of the day. For example, you could have a list on your door of all of the things you need to remember before leaving (such as keys, wallet, turning the heaters off...) or write a to do list first thing in the morning. Whiteboards tend to be great for this, as you can clearly plan out your priorities for the day first thing in the morning.

It is also helpful to have an evening routine, because people who have ADHD often suffer with sleep problems, as in 'S is for Sleep'. An evening routine can signal to your brain that it is ready to switch off and relax, setting you up for a good night's sleep. If we end our day on our phones, it's likely to keep our brains in the alert, restless mode that is not conducive to rest.

Activities that an evening routine could involve include:

- ❏ Switching off any technology one hour before going to sleep
- ❏ Having an allocated 'bed time' each night
- ❏ Meditating
- ❏ Yoga or another form of exercise
- ❏ Drinking a non-caffeinated drink at a certain time
- ❏ Eating dinner at a certain time
- ❏ Writing in a journal – gratitude diaries are particularly helpful
- ❏ Cleaning your room
- ❏ Reading

Think about what your ideal morning and evening routine would look like. Now, pick *one* of those things, for one time of day. To make a routine, it is more important that it is realistic for you to do over a long period of time to form a habit, rather than a grand routine that you will be able to stick to for a few days before feeling bad about forgetting to do it and giving up.

Write down the one thing that you would like to incorporate into your routine to start with, along with the exact time and length of times that you will be doing it for – make sure it is so small that it doesn't seem worth doing. For example, you may write down, 'meditate for one minute each morning'.

This tiny change will grow as you do it. If you can allow yourself to simply stick with one small task each day for a month, it will become a habit and prove to you that you *can* commit to a routine. You can then incorporate another task, or make it longer. The idea is to grow your routine over time and make it part of your framework. Watch out for anything that could be a potential blockage to your routine – for example, using an app on your phone to meditate. This will necessarily involve using your phone and mean that you waste time scrolling rather than meditating.

Finding an anchor

Think of your ADHD-mind like a helium filled balloon. Finding an anchor is something or someone who will hold your balloon down to the floor, so you don't fly off and pop in the sky. The above routine could certainly be an anchor, but another way that I have found particularly helpful to ground myself is having a dedicated person or 'thing' in my life to ground me.

This is essentially advance planning. It's finding something to commit to that you care about deeply, that you cannot easily give up and which will not give up on you, when the going gets tough. Having an anchor helps us remember why we are doing it in the first place, and to work through any difficulties. Marriage is a good example – it is voluntarily contractually binding yourself to a person so that it is harder to break up on a whim!

Other examples of anchors could be our best friends, therapists, pets, family, rental agreements and so on. They are the things that we have to put in effort for, such as waking up early to walk a dog on cold, dark mornings, but we do it because we ultimately love them – which does not change when things become stressful.

These anchors are what add to our identity and bring meaning to our lives. They are the cherry on top of the stable routine – bringing us a sense of security and self-worth. They should be unchanging, providing unconditional support. Think of the anchors like the neighbours for your scaffolding, as though you are a terraced house and they are either side of you.

It is important to remember to have a reciprocal relationship with your anchor. As we will see in 'L is for Love', ADHD-ers can sometimes encounter problems with people in their lives because of misunderstandings. The entire point of having a designated anchor is to have something or someone in your life that you care so much about, you will honour your responsibilities to them no matter what. These are two way relationships, even if your anchor is inanimate!

To identify an anchor, think about something or somebody in your life that is secure, solid and that you can trust. This could be a pet dog, your parents, the gym, a partner – anything at all! Write down who or what they are and the reasons behind them being your anchor.

You don't need to do anything else, but if you'd like to, maybe you would like to write a letter to your anchor. You could thank them for weighing you down with stability, acknowledge the benefits they bring to your life and your own commitments to them. You don't have to send it – they might not be able to read it!

However, if your anchor is a person, it could be helpful to have a conversation with them about your ADHD and explain to them the significance that they hold in your life, thanking them for it.

Mindfulness

Bringing yourself into the present moment is enormously helpful in terms of stress and waiting before you act on your thoughts. Some forms of it have been proven to help with ADHD symptoms (Mitchell JT, McIntyre EM, English JS, et al., 2017). Think of it like giving your brain a workout. There are many different methods of mindfulness as we will see in 'Z is for Zen', but a good starting off point is figuring out what makes you feel relaxed.

The typical 'non-moving' meditating can be difficult for people who have ADHD – sitting still is hard enough, let alone for long periods of time! Fortunately, there are lots of different kinds of meditation available – you just need to identify what stops your brain from incessant thinking.

For example, working out. As we saw in 'E is for Exercise', my brain can't think about anything else except not throwing up in high intensity gym classes! Yoga is a brilliant way to give your brain a rest as you concentrate on trying to get your foot behind your ear.

Other types of mindfulness that could be beneficial include walking meditation, running, painting, writing, reading – anything at all. The point of mindfulness is to bring your awareness to the present moment. There are several exercises that you can do in stressful situations to bring your awareness to what is happening in that moment and essentially distract your brain from thinking. For example, you could spot all of the objects around you that are a certain colour, or count your breaths.

Mindfulness is key for ADHD-ers to learn how to be their own anchor and ground themselves. Write down what this means for you and how you can incorporate this into your life – remember to keep it achievable and sustainable over a long period of time! Set yourself reminders to be present, such as post-it notes on your mirror or alarms on your phone throughout the day. Give your mind a rest - it is definitely well deserved.

is for high-functioning

Did you know?

- ADHD has been scientifically linked to the ability to 'hyper-focus' (Hupfeld, Abagis & Shah, 2019). This means episodes of long-lasting, highly-focused attention, which suggests that ADHD doesn't necessarily mean there is an attention 'deficit', but an unique way of paying attention.

- Having ADHD doesn't necessarily equate to not being objectively 'successful', and the success of those who are able to function 'well' in society (for example, by having successful careers) may mask the presence of ADHD. In October 2020, a psychiatrist was reported to have said, 'if he has managed to get to the 3rd year of a Law Degree, then presumably he does not have significant cognitive impairment, and it is not, of course, the duty of the local Mental Health Services to help him get a 2:1 degree in Law.'[7]

- It has been proven that adults with ADHD may succeed professionally despite significant symptoms of inattention and executive dysfunction (Palmini, 2008). Though they might appear objectively successful, this doesn't diminish their suffering any more than others with ADHD - in fact, they may be less likely to seek help, have incredibly low self-esteem and overcompensate in ways that could result in burnout.

One of the reasons that doctors consistently told me I was fine when I complained of my ADHD symptoms to them was because I was extremely high functioning. My ADHD

---

[7] https://twitter.com/mwjsimpson/status/1314982988250329089

manifests in ways that are not immediately apparent – I managed to get good exam results and graduate from university with a law degree, but I was plagued by constant bouts of anxiety, depression, hyperactivity and impulsive decisions that meant I was unable to commit to anything, and would periodically sabotage everything in my life. Underneath all of the outward-facing success, I was a mess.

As ADHD manifests differently for everyone, there is no typical ADHD-er. The hyperactive child disrupting the class may have ADHD as much as the one at the back staring out of the window. People who seem incredibly accomplished may suffer with crippling ADHD, despite being able to achieve and do many different things. From the outside, they may appear highly successful – particularly because our society celebrates productivity and being 'busy'.

Why is this a problem then?

It is a problem because though these people may be able to hold everything together on the outside, on the inside they may very well be struggling to cope from day to day. This is why we have more seemingly happy people committing suicide than ever before, because what looks like success on the outside does not necessarily translate inwards. It can be incredibly difficult to put your hands up and say that you have a problem, especially if you don't appear to have one to the people around you. The achievements themselves can be the coping strategy of such people, who tend to feel that they need to 'do' things in order to simply exist - they are human doings instead of human beings.

Hyper-focus: the hidden superpower of ADHD

A large part of why ADHD-ers may be extraordinarily high-functioning is to do with their ability to hyper-focus. This is how I graduated with a law degree, despite attending hardly any lectures because I was unable to listen - and falling asleep in the ones I did attend! I am able to hyper-focus on things that I am interested in - which is why this book is so important, because I figured out the way to make myself interested in the things that don't come naturally to me, unlocking my ADHD brain to work at its full potential.

Hyper-focus refers to an intense fixation on an interest or activity for an extended period of time and is commonly found in people who have ADHD. It is similar to being in a state of 'flow', which was described as being a state of 'intense concentration, energised attention, complete absorption in an activity that produces intense feelings of enjoyment.' (M. Csikszentmihalyi & I. S. Csikszentmihalyi, 1988)

It is *intense* – everything else in the world is blocked out to focus on this one thing. It's like binge watching an addictive TV series. I have had periods where I would wake up at 6am and work until 12am, hardly eating anything and not moving for the entire day - this is productive, but definitely not healthy!

One research participant described hyper-focus as, 'brain caviar... being able to channel all that random energy that's flying around in my head into one intense hyper-focused sort of beam...it's giving the brain a task that it's almost designed for'. They described the ADHD brain energy as being 'unfocused, quite scattered, chaotic and a bit random, but give that brain something that you can really tune into... I get this incredible intense con concentration and that's great for work'. (Miranda et al , 2012)

This is quite ironic when ADHD stands for a 'deficit' of attention. I would say that the attention system of ADHD-ers is dysregulated rather than defective – if we want to focus on something, we might be able to much more effectively than a neurotypical person would be able to. It's just that we don't always have much choice about what we want to focus on, and our brains refuse to focus on things we aren't interested in - wanting and choosing do not come from the same part of us. We can *want* to eat ice cream for breakfast, but we *choose* to eat cereal. So whilst writing an entire book in a week might be achievable for someone with ADHD, tasks such as washing up or taking out the rubbish may be a completely different story.

People who have ADHD can be referred to as lazy, which is something I have been called throughout my life. Part of the relief of being diagnosed with ADHD is understanding that you are *not lazy*. Your brain simply does not focus in the same way that other people's do. Hyper-focus is thought to result from abnormally low levels of dopamine, which makes it difficult to 'shift gears' to do the boring but necessary tasks - or anything that isn't your focus of the moment. It can feel like having a superpower, but it is also generally quite unhealthy, exhausting and annoying - it needs to be regulated.

The trick of hacking your ADHD is figuring out how to shift the gears and spread the hyper-focus across things equally, and how to trick yourself into *wanting* to do things that you don't really want to do – as we saw in 'E is for Exercise', for example. Once you understand your hyper-focus and what drives your high-functioning ADHD, you can learn to train it.

This may require external stimulation, such as timers and alarm clocks. Calendars, to do lists, written visual reminders and physical signals such as vibrating fitness watches are great ways of both training yourself to do a task you don't really want to do, and to take breaks from hyper-focusing on a task.

Think of yourself like a child that needs to be convinced into doing things they don't want to do, such as eating broccoli. You might disguise the broccoli as chips or play an aeroplane game with it, or let the child watch TV afterwards if they eat it. It might seem silly to think of yourself in this way, particularly if you are a super successful high-flyer, but try to get in touch with your inner child that simply *does not want to do the boring things.*

Another challenge people with high-functioning ADHD may have is refusing to acknowledge that they need help. When I started taking ADHD medication, after a week or so I felt that I was 'cured' and could stop taking the tablets. Being your own doctor is not a good idea, as seen in 'M is for Medication'. In therapy I would completely ignore the therapist, listing my problems and analysing them all myself, stating how I needed to fix them. We are used to fixing problems and operating at 100 miles per hour, living at a rate of 150%. It is very difficult to slow down, and in our 'weaker' moments we might ask for help, before reverting straight back to motor-mode and brushing off the plea for help as being 'emotional'.

The high-functioning ADHD-er tends to hold themselves to an extremely high standard of perfection. They tend to appear extremely confident as they hold up this perfect exterior to the world, shooting from appointment to appointment, managing everything at once. On the inside, they tend to be terrified of one thing falling down, of stopping even for a second – or everything will come crashing down.

I think of it like the adult-life equivalent of tidying your bedroom by shoving all of the mess in your wardrobe and living in fear that somebody will open the wardrobe. Everything looks neat and tidy, until the wardrobe explodes.

Another problem that accompanies high-functioning ADHD is boredom. The impulsive thoughts and poor attention span that accompanies ADHD can manifest in a high achiever as constantly starting and quitting projects, along with very harsh self-criticism. It can also result in an inability to sit still or relax and be quite exhausting for the people around us! Having a 'Type-A' personality can contribute to appearing as though you are quitting things because you simply don't care, especially if you start things with intense enthusiasm and deliver on the initial goals, before falling short as your brain simply refuses to engage anymore. I have encountered a lot of difficulties in relationships over the years from continuously cancelling plans and projects as a result of becoming frustrated and bored.

This also ties in with being a people pleaser, as we will see in 'N is for No'. People with high-functioning ADHD may struggle with the concept of saying no to anything, thinking of themselves like a superhero who should be able to do anything. This usually means being far too overcommitted and prioritising other people before yourself, often resulting in burnout as in 'B is for Burnout'.

In my opinion, the best thing that a person with ADHD can do is learn how to hack their own mind - once you can decide what you want to focus on, it's truly amazing to see how much ADHD can be a gift.

How to train your hyper-focus

1. Try to think of a time that you have hyper-focused on something in your life. This could be anything from a project you were particularly interested in, to a book that you couldn't put down.

2. Write down the reasons why you were hyper-focused, what made you interested on that occasion – your 'hyper-focus triggers'. What was it about the situation that you were particularly interested in? People with ADHD tend to react to novelty, external stimulation (such as deadlines) and excitement.

3. Try to identify the feelings you had when you were hyper-focusing. What did you miss out on whilst hyper-focusing – what were the negatives associated with it? What typically happens after a period of hyper-focusing?

4. Write down three ways that you can manage your hyper-focus when it next occurs, such as designating breaks by setting alarms or making a sustainable plan as in 'T for Time Management'.

5. Write down three things that you wish you could hyper-focus on, such as cleaning. Now, find a way of applying your 'hyper-focus triggers' to these activities – you may have to use your imagination! For example, you could think of a game to clean as much as possible in 5 minute bursts to your favourite songs.

Tips

- Remember that your 75% is the equivalent to most people's 100% in terms of effort level. See 'G is for Grounding' for tips on how to calm the complex machine that is your mind.

- Be kind to yourself. Check out 'N is for No' on tips for how to prioritise yourself and stop automatically saying yes.

- Try to give yourself some free time each week, even if it is just half an hour of doing nothing at all - without your phone. This time is necessary for you to relax.

- Implement phone-free hours whenever you can. Give your mind a rest!

- Declutter your phone and clear out any apps you don't need.

- Make sure that you have 8 hours of sleep per night. Sleep is very important for managing ADHD symptoms, as in 'S is for Sleep'. Turn off any electronic devices an hour before going to sleep and charge them in a different room.

- Try to separate your work and personal life. Set yourself a maximum time to be at work, say 7pm, and make sure that you leave. Try to disconnect your work emails from your phone and establish a boundary between the two worlds.

- Make time to see a therapist. It is so valuable to speak to someone that you don't have to keep up a perfect front with and who can just accept you for the imperfectly perfect person that you are behind all of the 'doing'.

❑ Break tasks down into tiny steps. High-functioning ADHD can often gloss over the details which generally build up in the mental cupboard, waiting to burst. Try to make an effort to set realistic deadlines, with more time than you think you need, and to take things slowly.

❑ Remember that you do not need to do everything. You are a human being and do not have to meet some insanely high standard of living. You have a right to be happy, relax, and enjoy just 'being', not doing!

❑ Remember that being diagnosed with ADHD, taking medication or receiving any kind of help in managing your ADHD symptoms will not negatively impact your productivity levels. It will actually make you *more* productive, as you can choose to channel your high-functioning energy in a sustainable, effective way – and enjoy your life!

is for interests

Did you know?

- Adults with ADHD are often looking for stimulation, novelty and excitement, because when we are interested in something, the executive functions of the brain click into gear and work well. When we are interested in something, it is much easier to focus - and much more difficult when not!

- High novelty seeking and low self-directedness have been scientifically associated with the personality of a person with ADHD (Perroud et al, 2016). This could explain why ADHD-ers may feel interested in a lot of new things but become bored easily, and move onto something else. In turn, this can result in low self-esteem and feelings of failure, as in 'W is for Weaknesses'.

- ADHD has been scientifically linked to high creativity levels (White & Shah , 2011). If ADHD-ers can understand their own creative potential and interests, then this can help to identify careers that may be particularly suitable to their strengths and interests, as in 'J is for Jobs'.

A common difficulty for people who have ADHD is figuring out what they are passionate about. This is quite ironic, because they tend to be passionate about lots of different things – but just have trouble sustaining that interest one the initial thrill wears off.

The reason this is so significant for ADHD-ers is because we are motivated by interest. We tend to enthusiastically arrange our lives around our interests, which is exhausting and upsetting when we inevitably lose interest after a period of time. As in the 'B is for Burnout' chapter, we tend to throw ourselves into our interest-of-the-moment with an intense passion and dedication... which can often involve purchasing some new equipment, uniform or membership, as in 'F is for Finance'.

Not only is this expensive, but it holds up the stories of being unable to commit to anything and cycles of self-hate and guilt. We find a new hobby, throw ourselves into it and tell everyone we know about this new course we have signed up to. Once the high wears off, and the reality hits of having to put in sustained effort, we quit. We might have cupboards filled with dusty instruments, forgotten uniforms, dried up art supplies... sound familiar?

It can also be difficult to figure out how much effort we should dedicate to our interests, for example, in choosing a career path. When we are interested in a lot of different things, it can be overwhelming to try and figure out how to translate this into 'normal' life, to have a balance of interests and things that we enjoy doing instead of just one at a time.

Interests are what keep life interesting, but they do not need to be our reason for living or sole means of survival. When we try to make them so, it sets us up for failure. We are human beings who live an extremely long time, and what we were interested in as a child, we won't necessarily be doing as adults. Interests and hobbies are supposed to come and go, they aren't meant to be the **only** thing we will do for the rest of our life.

As in 'J is for Jobs', there are a variety of different factors relevant to finding the right one for you that surpass interest alone. Finding a 'good enough' job - one that you are interested in, but is not your *core reason for living to the exclusion of anything else* is perfectly reasonable. I previously had done more jobs than I care to remember for absolutely no payment whatsoever, because I was really interested in the work. This is fine if you are just there for the learning experience, but if you are building up companies and working for free then you may be being exploited.

It's helpful to think of your interests like a tree, with the trunk as your job, providing the stability. If a job can provide you with a certain amount of guilt-free money and time to chase interests outside of work, then you can will be able to enjoy these interests much better than if you were basing your entire life off them, with far less pressure to 'succeed'.

Acknowledge and accept that you are a creative, enthusiastic person with a lust for life and learning, and that not everything is going to stick – nor does it have to. We can't all become Olympic athletes but we can try out every class in the gym with no commitment attached. We can accept the child inside of us that wants to try out every single class in the world. It's fine to let them do that, but with boundaries in place to protect them from setting up their own gym and bankrupting themselves. Remember that it is completely fine to quit something, as we will see in 'Q is for Quitting'.

There is a book called *'Refuse to Choose'* by Barbara Sher, which talks about 'scanners' - people who are simply interested in lots of different things. Barbara says that we should celebrate all of our half-finished accomplishments, and can file them all away with a plan for somebody to come along and finish them off one day. The book emphasises how amazing it is to have so many interests and passions, and that when we stop being interested in them, simply means we have taken what we needed from that particular hobby.

It can also feel very difficult to know what you are interested in, so you might end up doing nothing at all. It's vital for ADHD-ers to have interests - they are the fuel for a curious life and keep our brains engaged. If you're feeling uninspired and as though you're not interested in anything, give yourself a day where you don't use your phone. You'll end up doing *something* - follow your curiosity!

I advise keeping a journal where you can write down all of your ideas and interests as they pop up, so you don't feel the need to act fully on them immediately - they are there when you need them.

How to manage your interests

1. Write down a list of 3 of each your past and current hobbies. If you're going through an uninspired patch, write down a list of everything that you are vaguely interested in – even if it's just 'chocolate' or 'reading'.

2. Think about anything these interests might have in common – do they involve other people or being alone? Are they high energy, or are they relaxing?

3. Identify your interest levels for these hobbies: why did you start it, when did it feel most exciting, and how did it end?

4. Identify the side-effects that each of these hobbies has caused you. How much have you spent on the hobby, for example? What emotions have they left you with?

5. You should now be able to spot what triggers your interest in and out of something. Write down your triggers, which should be able to provide warning flags to you to help balance that passion see-saw.

6. Write down some boundaries that you can implement to help sustain your interest at a healthy level, as long as you want to. These should complement the 'out of interest' triggers, for example committing to not financially investing in an activity any more than necessary until you have done it for one month, or ensuring that you have enough time to rest in the week.

is for jobs

Did you know?

- People with untreated ADHD are twice as likely to have been fired from a job than people without ADHD (Barkley, 1988).

- If ADHD impacts a person significantly in their daily life, it can be seen as a disability under the Equality Act 2010, meaning that employers have a duty to protect employees from discrimination and make reasonable adjustments for them to do their jobs where necessary. The UK Government may be able to help fund these adjustments, such as a job coach, through a scheme called Access to Work.

- Studies have shown that certain ADHD traits, such as hyper-focus may benefit entrepreneurs (Wiklund, Patzelt & Dimov , 2016). Research has shown that ADHD-ers have outperformed people without ADHD by generating more creative ideas and being more likely to find a correct solution to a problem - they have been shown to be highly creative, divergent thinkers and excellent problem solvers (Born to Be ADHD, 2017).

Finding and keeping a job can be very difficult for a person with ADHD. This is largely because we find it difficult to sustain our attention on activities that we are not interested in – and all jobs have parts that are more interesting than others. On the other end of the scale, doing something we *are* particularly interested in can lead to burnout, as in 'B is for Burnout', that can unfortunately result in a person with ADHD steam-rolling into a company with lots of grand ideas, before steam rolling out again a few months later.

ADHD can also clash with the bureaucracy of organisations, given our aversion to details and administrative tasks. We may also have to work closely alongside others on a daily basis, which can be difficult for ADHD-ers who are hyper-sensitive to rejection and prone to emotional dysregulation. For example, impulsively acting out after a difficult conversation can result in leaving a job without thinking it through properly.

Environments such as offices may also not be the best working environments for a person with ADHD to thrive, with background chats and endless opportunities for us to become distracted. As in 'Y is for Your Body', ADHD can result in sensory issues such as a strong aversion to smells - which could lead to unexpected outbursts when these build up, such as colleagues microwaving their lunches!

This isn't even to mention the stress of finding a job in itself. Which is difficult enough for everyone, let alone those with ADHD who struggle with forms and processes. Speaking of ADHD, would that be declared as a disability on the application form? It is a minefield of bureaucracy and confidence-testers, which can seem never-ending.

ADHD-ers may find self-employment to work better for them. However, with a lack of self-esteem and confidence, this can result in not reaching our full potential, or failing due to a lack of structure to support us. We might undersell ourselves, or avoid vitally important parts of running a business, such as accounts, because we simply can't process it. The freedom of being self-employed should be weighed carefully against the stability and routine of having a full time job - different options may suit different people. Understanding ourselves is the first step in figuring out what works best for us in terms of employment.

Good jobs for ADHD-ers

It might be difficult to figure out what kind of job to do if you have ADHD, because we have a tendency to want to do *everything* - but its difficult to know what the 'reality' of a job is like without trying it out. As a rough guide, the below elements may be good to incorporate into your career:

- Passion: as ADHD-ers are often motivated by our interests and emotions, it's good to find a job that you feel passionate about, that have a *purpose* behind them. Finding our 'why' means that we always have something to inspire us, even when things become difficult. Examples could include charity work, social work, teaching, or working with animals - or whatever your passion is.

- Adrenaline: the ADHD mind is often seeking stimulation, adrenaline and excitement - we tend to be good in a crisis. We can thrive in challenging, fast-paced jobs that are motivated by a highly intense external environment. Examples could include being a paramedic, fire-fighter, working in the police force, surgeon, stockbroker, skydiving instructor or barrister - the list is endless!

- Variety: jobs where every day is different will help prevent us from getting bored. For example, jobs where you meet new people every day, such as being a barista, retail work, client-facing work such as being a therapist or customer service, to name a few.

- Creativity: ADHD has been linked to high creativity levels, and creativity tends to spark happiness! Examples could include being an actor, artist, dancer, writer, designer or musician.

- Problem solving: people with ADHD tend to be good at this, and it's good for our 'out of the box' thinking to be valued in our work. For example, by being an IT specialist, working in technology, product design or as a consultant.

- Movement: for ADHD-ers with a lot of energy, as in 'Y is for Your Body', physical jobs may suit us very well. These could include working as an athlete, fitness trainer, waiter or waitress, tour guide or hairdresser.

How to find a job that you want to do

1. If you are unsure what job you want to do, pick something that is of interest to you (see 'I is for Interests'), or the job that appeals most from the examples above! Research the different types of jobs available in this field.

2. Write down a list of (a) skills that you are good at, (b) things you enjoy doing and (c) your top 3 values in terms of work, in order. You might not know what these are yet, which is fine, but try to think about what is important to you. Online personality quizzes can help with this.

3. Look at your lists and try to identify jobs within them. You essentially want to match your skills with your interests and priorities. Once you have a fairly good

idea of what this looks like, then look at your network. Ask friends of friends if they know of anyone in the industry you want to work in, or send out polite messages on Linkedin asking for a quick phone call or coffee meet-up to find out more about the role. Have a look at your CV and edit it to the specific job that you are applying for.

4. Depending on your situation, try to gain work experience in the industry that you want to work for, or apply for a job suitable to your skill level and experience. Make sure that this job is realistic and achievable – for example, don't waste your time applying for a role that is far higher than your skill level. If this is in a field of self-employment, shadowing people and asking them to mentor you is a really good way of learning what the job requires.

5. It is up to you whether you feel that ADHD is a disability to be declared when applying for a job. If you need reasonable adjustments, for example, extra time to sit a written test, or could end up being late, then it is worth mentioning. If you think that it is not relevant to your performance in an interview, then it may not be - it is a personal decision.

Disclosing your ADHD at work

Under the Equality Act 2010, you are disabled if you have a physical or mental impairment that has a 'substantial' and 'long-term' negative effect on your ability to do normal daily activities. This is a tricky thing to decide and deeply dependent on the individual. In my personal opinion, if you are coming up against struggles directly relating to your ADHD, I would recommend declaring it to your workplace.

There are pros and cons to declaring your ADHD at work, and there might not always be an obvious opportunity to do so, but that doesn't mean that you necessarily shouldn't. Even if you initially don't disclose it at first, you can later on - you might not realise how it can impact you before doing a job, or until you are encountering work-related stress. Not only will disclosure help protect you from potential discrimination related to your disability, but it should also mean that you and your employer hopefully have a more transparent and effective relationship, in addition to potentially resulting in you being better able to do your job.

On the other hand, it can feel embarrassing to do so, and as we know, there is a lot of stigma about ADHD. 82% of respondents to an ADDitude survey said they had not asked for workplace accommodations, and more than half hadn't disclosed their ADHD to their employer (ADDitude, 2020). Each person will have to weigh up the pros and cons of their own individual situation.

This is understandable, given the shame one could feel in having to 'declare' a 'disability' in relation to their job - but it's important to remember that **this is not your fault.** You have a neurodevelopmental condition that means you think differently to others, which isn't a bad thing, but can mean that you are subject to expectations that you simply might not be able to meet. In many ways having ADHD means that you are bringing unique strengths to the job, as in 'W is for Weaknesses', and your employer has a duty to help you with any difficulties you might encounter.

ADHD might not always feel like a disability, but it definitely can be. Just because it is invisible, doesn't mean that it doesn't severely impact your life. By having the reasonable adjustments that you need made, you are simply being accommodated to be able to be do your job as equally as your colleagues are able to.

The process of disclosing your ADHD at work will be different for everybody depending on their circumstances. I would recommend asking your doctor for advice on your particular situation, and if you decide to disclose it to your employer, then finding the Human Resources department. They might refer you to an external 'Occupational Therapist' to receive advice on how they can best accommodate your ADHD at work, such as with flexible working hours or working from a quieter part of the office.

If you are self-employed, you may not have anybody to disclose to! There are many different scenarios, but for those living in the UK, a Government scheme called Access to Work is available to help people with disabilities stay in employment, including self-employment. There is an online application, usually followed by a conversation with an independent assessor who will talk about reasonable adjustments you may need, and then a decision is made. The Government can fund these adjustments for you - even if you are employed - and they can be truly life changing.

How to work through blockages

As we've seen, people with ADHD may struggle staying in employment - especially when things become stressful. We might have difficulty with becoming distracted and procrastinating (see 'P is for Procrastination') managing our time ('T is for Time Management'), organisation ('O is for Organisation'), boredom ('I is for Interests'), maintaining relationships ('L is for Love'), rejection ('R is for Rejection') and impulsivity ('G is for Grounding'!). The good news is that there are ways around all of these challenges - we might just have to do a bit of advance planning!

1. Understand your blockages at work. Write down the things that have caused you to quit jobs in the past, or what you imagine could cause you to leave this job, such as conflicts with colleagues or setting unrealistic expectations for yourself.

2. Tackle your blockages. Write down ways that you can actively target these in advance of them becoming a problem, or ways that your employer could possibly help.

    Some examples could include:

    ❑ Wearing noise-cancelling headphones in the office, asking to sit in a quiet area or for flexible working hours / locations so that you can concentrate.

    ❑ Writing out what you want to say in meetings before attending them, which can help in not becoming flustered under pressure in meetings and staying organised.

    ❑ Having clear charts of work each week to visibly see the stages of different projects and maintain structure, for example, on a whiteboard or wall planner.

    ❑ Asking for help from colleagues for areas that you might struggle in, such as data handling.

- ❏ Finding out whether your employer has any mental health support policies in place for employees, such as therapy or mindfulness sessions.

- ❏ Setting yourself deadlines for work in your calendar to give a sense of urgency, especially for projects that don't have clear time frames.

- ❏ Taking regular breaks and ensuring that you always eat lunch!

Try to set yourself some 'minimum goals', such as staying in a job for a period of time before quitting, even if you don't like it at first. Remember that you don't have to stay there forever - it's just trying it out, and every experience teaches us something new.

3. Implement your plans and decide whether you want to declare your ADHD to your employer. A great way of starting a conversation about mental health in the workplace and for stressful periods is making use of the Wellness Action Plans by the organisation Mind.

   These are documents which everyone in a team would fill out, writing down how they best cope with stress, what might trigger them to feel worse, and how their colleagues can help. They're an excellent reminder that mental health affects us all - regardless of having ADHD or not. There is also a plan for working from home, which is particularly important as this becomes more common, making us less physically connected to our colleagues, who are an important support system in times of stress.

Self-employment

Many people who have ADHD flourish in self-employment, as they are their own bosses and able to work as they wish. If you struggle with fitting into a 'box' then it can be enormously freeing to be completely in control of your own career, however, it's important to acknowledge areas where you could need help and to get that help!

There are a few important factors to remember when working for yourself with ADHD:

- ❑ When considering becoming self-employed, try to think as long-term as possible. Some jobs can be great for us to do whilst we figure out what to do, but it's ideal to have a career that will give you a sense of stability. It can be very helpful to work with a coach, for example, to ensure that you are as organised as possible.

- ❑ Try to avoid spending large amounts of money until you are absolutely sure about your chosen career. Being self-employed requires a strong sense of financial skill, and being able to save money, as you will generally pay tax at the end of the year! It's a good idea to work with a financial advisor or accountant to ensure that this is taken care of.

- ❑ Ensure that you have a routine that you stick to, with clear goals and accountability. Being self-employed means that you are your own boss, which requires a strong sense of self-regulation! 'G is for Grounding' can help with this.

❑ Remember that it is ok to ask for help and to delegate. Running a business all by yourself is incredibly difficult, and it is important to have someone to hand, even if it is just to offload your stresses onto. You cannot do everything, no matter how hard you try. I would really advise looking at Government support schemes for self-employed people and disabilities, such as Access to Work - that's what they're there for!

Working from home

More people than ever before are working from home, which can be a blessing and a curse for ADHD-ers. This became more prevalent during the Covid-19 pandemic, and is likely to stick around.

If you have ADHD and are working from home, it's good to do an assessment of your work set-up to see if it can be improved. By working from home, we are in control of our time and space a lot more than we would be in an office type situation.

Some important considerations are:

- Your home office. Assess how you tend to work most days - where you typically would sit, the types of chairs, tables and screens you might be using. It's good to be working in a place specifically designated as being for work, if possible, to help your mind shift gears. Also important is to invest in proper equipment such as an office chair, to ensure you aren't straining your back - as in 'Y is for Your Body', we may not always be aware of discomfort in our body. For ADHD-ers, it's generally good to be working in a place that has minimal distractions.

- Your working hours - do these work for you? Are you working more or less than you normally would in an office?

- Any routines that you have throughout the day. These include what you do when first waking up and going to sleep, and any breaks that you might have. They are really important for us when working from home, as they help to bring a sense of structure to an otherwise potentially unstructured day, without the ordinary 'getting ready' time and commutes to and from work. For more on routines, see 'G is for Grounding'.

- How often you are taking breaks, and what you do in them. Screens are not great for our health, and it can be very easy for ADHD-ers to be hyper-focused on their work without taking any breaks for the entire day. If this is you, look at how you can implement breaks, which are vital for our mental health. Some ideas could include setting an alarm, visual reminders such as on a whiteboard, or arranging to meet a friend at a certain time each day.

- How often you are exercising. This is really important, because exercise is hugely helpful to managing the symptoms of ADHD, as seen in 'E is for Exercise'. However, it can be difficult enough for us to force ourselves to exercise, without our ordinary routines of going to the gym after work, for example, being taken away. Try to make sure that you are at least going outside once a day and find a gym class that you can incorporate into working from home, such as online yoga classes in the morning. Ones where you are on screen tend to be best for ADHD-ers - if I have my camera turned off, I tend to become distracted by all of the things that need doing in my room!

- Any distractions that pop up during your working day and things that could help with this. For example, I put my phone in a specified box during certain hours of the day so that I can focus, and try to avoid working in the same room as my housemates when I have a very busy day. Working from home is also a good opportunity to use things you may not be able to in an office, such as a large whiteboard to write down your priorities for the day!

- How often you are seeing and speaking to other people. It can be very lonely working from home, which can contribute to feelings of anxiety in seeing people again, when we become used to being alone. Try to factor in time spent with other people when you can into your weeks, even if it's just a chat with colleagues or a call with your family. Human connection is really important for all of us to maintain, especially when we are becoming less physically connected.

If working from home is very difficult for you, consider signing up to a co-working space, or a couple of days a week working from a cafe. The benefits of this new way of working is that we can adapt it to what works best for us, instead of having to fit into a certain office-shaped box!

is for kindness

Did you know?

- It has been proven that people with ADHD suffer from levels of low self-esteem (Mazzone et al, 2013).

- It has been estimated that by age 12, children who have ADHD receive 20,000 more negative messages from parents, teachers and other adults than their non-ADHD peers (Dodson).

- ADHD has been linked with a high risk of self-harm and suicide (Conjero et al., 2019), particularly for adolescent girls (American Psychological Association (APA), 2012).

In my experience people who have ADHD tend to be extremely kind and compassionate to others. The constant buzzing and overthinking in their brain often revolves around other people and making sure they are alright, and they can prioritise everyone else except themselves.

Whilst this compassion is a wonderful quality to have, it can cause several problems. As seen in 'N is for No', people-pleasing is commonly associated with ADHD and can result in feelings of exhaustion and loneliness. The compassion combined with our quick-thinking minds, enthusiasm for problem-solving and passion for those we love can sometimes also result in offering advice which is not wanted or needed, and can have the opposite effect to helping somebody, which we see more of in 'L is for Love'.

This can be confusing and frustrating for someone who just wants to help others. It can be very difficult when you are trying your best to be 'nice' in the hope of being liked, accepted and valued by others, and you feel repeatedly rejected for this.

It is almost a distortion of kindness, because we are notoriously terrible at being kind to ourselves. As when a plane is crashing, you must put your own oxygen mask on first before helping others.

A therapist once asked me what my priorities were in life, and I had no idea. My own priorities didn't register at all on the list. I used to be so willing to help anyone at all in the hope of being liked that I was surrounded by toxic people who used me. I thought it was selfish and bad to help yourself, to think of yourself over another person. I was kind to everybody but myself.

ADHD can result in impulsive, self-destructive behaviour. Not thinking things through before acting and chasing adrenaline can result in risky decisions. This is combined with the emotional effects of having ADHD – of being hyper-sensitive to rejection, of feeling like a failure and unable to commit to anything, of beating yourself up for not being able to do simple tasks or for viewing the world differently to everybody else.

So this chapter is about being kind to yourself and beating the self-destructive thinking. Recognising that you have a right to have your needs met and to be happy is imperative to managing your ADHD symptoms effectively, and in turn, helps the people around you. The people in your life who deserve to be there would much prefer you to be happy looking after yourself rather than unhappy and trying to look after them. When you are your own priority, you will think more about how flippant decisions can affect your long-term happiness. You will prioritise looking after yourself, training yourself to the boring-but-necessary tasks, organising your life ahead of time, implementing structure and stability. You will choose to beat the negative side effects of ADHD and learn how to utilise it for your benefit.

Everybody's happiness is their own responsibility. If you are not kind to yourself, you cannot rely on other people to be. It can be extremely difficult to change the way that you think about yourself, because this may be what your life is built up on. Stories of being unworthy, not good enough, unable to commit. You have to burn right through these stories to the underlying problem and recognise that you are good enough.

Remember the baby deserving of love for no other reason than it is alive, as seen in 'C is for Confidence'? You are deserving of love, happiness and acceptance without doing anything at all. You do not have to do anything to be liked by other people, and I guarantee that you have people in your life who love you unconditionally.

A large part of being kind to yourself is re-parenting yourself, as seen in 'O is for Organisation'. Nobody explains to us that when we leave home, we should start parenting ourselves – making sure that we eat healthy, regular meals, live in reasonably clean surroundings, get ourselves to all of our appointments on time and so on. There are basic human needs that we must meet for ourselves: food, water, air, safety, shelter, sleep.

This might sound simple in theory, but in practice this could be quite different. How good are you at cooking, or ensuring that you eat three healthy meals a day? How much water do you drink? How often do you take the time to breathe mindfully? How often do you engage in risky behaviour that puts you in danger – such as getting blackout drunk or taking drugs? How about cleaning your house or paying all the bills on time? How's your sleep? How equal are your relationships with others?

The great news is that by reading this book, you have already started being kind to yourself. Even taking the time to learn more about ADHD, whether you have it or not, indicates that you are open to the possibility of it existing. Recognising and accepting you may have ADHD is a huge first step in treating yourself with self-compassion.

Having ADHD provides an explanation for the things you might beat yourself up about, such as not being able to do your clothes washing until you have literally nothing left to wear. Accepting that you have been suffering with a neurodevelopmental condition for possibly your entire life, changes the foundations on which you have been living. It is not your fault. There is nothing you have done that has 'given' you ADHD.

By accepting this, you can choose to educate yourself and make changes accordingly that will help you to live a happier life. It can be terrifying, when you are only used to darkness, to give yourself the hope of living a life where your happiness is your own priority.

Further on from your basic survival needs, there are those which relate to your happiness. Yale university has a class called 'The Science of Well-being', (available on Coursera for free at the time of writing), which identifies scientifically proven, key factors to our happiness. These are: meditation, gratitude, savouring, kindness, connection, exercise, sleep and goals.

How are you at taking time for yourself and appreciating the simple things, as in 'Z is for Zen'? How much of your life do you really *live* – fully using your senses, such as eating a piece of cake and fully enjoying how good it tastes? How often are you kind to others with zero expectations in return? How often do you connect with the people around you and show up as yourself in your interactions? How about exercise, as in 'E is for Exercise'? How many hours of sleep do you have a night? What long-term goals are you working on?

Please don't be satisfied with just surviving. Choose to live a happy life, to enjoy the time that we have here on this planet. Life is short, and above all, you are deserving of the kindness that you give to others.

How to be kind to yourself

1. Honestly assess yourself in the below areas:
   - ❏ **Sleep** (how many hours you sleep per night, how tired you feel throughout the day)
   - ❏ **Eating** (how much you eat in a day, what kind of food you are eating)
   - ❏ **Mindfulness** (how often you take the time to be still, such as meditating, journaling or yoga)
   - ❏ **Health** (how much alcohol / drugs you consume, how healthy you feel in general)
   - ❏ **Exercise** (how often you exercise, the reasons why you exercise)
   - ❏ **Home** (how clean is your home, how stable is your home life?)

- ☐ **Finances** (how often are bills paid on time, do you save money?)
- ☐ **Social life** (how connected you feel to your friends, family or partner, how lonely you feel)
- ☐ **Hobbies** (how much interest in you have in your hobbies, how much you enjoy them)
- ☐ **Physical appearance** (how you feel about how you look, anything you would like to change)
- ☐ **Work** (how much you enjoy your job, what you may prefer to be doing)
- ☐ **Happiness** (overall, how happy you feel with your life at the moment)

2. Notice how you speak to yourself. Go back over the above list and try to spot if you spoke about yourself in a negative way, and note it down, along with any other observations you may have had from assessing your general happiness.

3. Write down the reasons why you may not have been kind to yourself in the past.

4. Write down the OPPOSITE to your statements above. For example, if you have written 'I am too lazy to cook myself a healthy meal', write 'I am NOT lazy.' Find all of the proof for the opposite statement. In our example this could include, 'I get out of bed every morning, have a job, and go to the gym'.

5. Go through the list again and write down how you can improve your happiness in each of the areas – what would be an act of kindness to yourself? Are there any

practical steps you can take from identifying the barriers of being kind to yourself? For example, could you go to sleep earlier, or stay off social media if you find yourself comparing yourself to others? Could you invest more time in what you are interested in, or cut out toxic people who make you feel unhappy?

6. Commit to being kind to yourself and implementing some of the actions above. Make sure steps are achievable, realistic and sustainable at first, but try to set yourself reminders to be kind to yourself, such as reminders on your phone. Some further examples of things you could do to be kind to yourself include:

- ❑ Notice every time you are mean to yourself, either in your head or out loud. Try to catch yourself out and apologise to yourself, changing the statement to be kind to yourself.

- ❑ Ask a friend to call you out every time you say something bad about yourself.

- ❑ Write yourself a love letter, as often as you can.

- ❑ Acknowledge all of the brilliant things about you. Try to give yourself three compliments every day, maybe starting a compliment journal!

- ❑ Celebrate every act of kindness to yourself, however small. Really savour and appreciate when you do something nice for yourself, such as cooking yourself a healthy meal. Take the time to notice how different you feel as a result and appreciate the time and effort you put in to yourself.

- ❏ Stop people pleasing! Some people in your life may be unhappy with you suddenly prioritising yourself instead of them and those are the ones who are likely to be exploiting your kindness. No is your new favourite word – see 'N is for No'.

- ❏ If you can, allocate some time to yourself each month to do something just for you. You could take yourself out on a date, such as going for a long walk in the park, ordering your favourite meal, or getting a massage. Whatever it is, make sure it leaves you feeling happy!

Did you know?

- Studies have proven that adult ADHD is associated with difficulties in social relationships and poor negation skills (Moya et al, 2014).
- Children with untreated or poorly controlled ADHD are more than 5 times more likely to participate in fights.
- About 70% of adults reported problems with anger or emotion as part of their ADHD (Nigg, 2020).

ADHD can have a huge impact on personal relationships. This chapter focuses primarily on platonic love with friends and family, as opposed to romantic love, which is discussed in 'X is for X-rated'.

The impulsive, self-destructive behaviour that ADHD-ers may be prone to can frustrate the people who care about them, especially when combined with emotional dysregulation and a difficulty in paying attention over a sustained period of time. This can result in people thinking that the person with ADHD does not care about the relationship. It can be difficult to sustain a two-way, equal relationship with someone who is 100% energy or nothing at all.

ADHD-ers are also prone to Rejection Sensitive Dysphoria ('RSD'), which is extreme emotional sensitivity and pain triggered by the perception of rejection, which we will discuss further in 'R is for Rejection'. This can be very problematic in relationships where we perceive to be being rejected or disliked - there is a tendency to catastrophize and to have black-or-white thinking in such situations.

Having ADHD can be incredibly lonely. It is very difficult for other people to understand you if they do not have full awareness or acceptance of ADHD, especially if you are not diagnosed. It can be hard for someone to believe that you physically cannot listen to them for an extended period of time, no matter how hard you try. Or that you literally cannot bring yourself to look at your bank account, clean your bedroom, or keep track of your appointments. For a person without ADHD, these are simply matters of 'motivation'. ADHD-ers might often find themselves being referred to as lazy by frustrated people in their life, who don't understand that this is a serious medical condition.

ADHD can also appear as rudeness, with a tendency to speak before we think. We might be prone to saying things that we don't mean or interrupt others. We may have bad memories because we can't focus on conversations properly, which in turn leads to forgetting appointments with others and asking questions we've already been told the answers to. This can result in general annoyance from others, who may believe that we don't care about them – when it is often quite the opposite in reality, as our brains are busy trying to avoid any potential rejection from someone we care about very much indeed.

In my experience, ADHD-ers don't deal particularly well with silence, and may blurt out conversation to fill any gaps in conversation, in the hope of making the other person feel comfortable. As in 'K is for Kindness', people who have ADHD are often extremely compassionate towards others, sometimes at the expense of themselves. This compassion is largely lost in translation as it may manifest as talking excessively about ourselves (because we don't know what to say) or unwanted advice. We tend to be good at seeing things from different perspectives, particularly having experienced pain ourselves, and thinking creatively, so our offers of help can often be well founded – but not always appropriately delivered.

This excessive talking can also often result in oversharing with others. ADHD-ers can struggle with boundaries and understanding what is and is not appropriate to share with another person. Whilst this is often done with the best of intentions to be open and honest, it can actually cause disjointed, unequal relationships as the other person knows far more about your life than you know about theirs. An important lesson for ADHD-ers is that trust is earned, not automatically granted, and you should only share personal information with people that you trust and who you feel have earned the right to hear it.

Oversharing in the hope of being honest and vulnerable is actually doing the opposite – you are hoping that by laying out all of your 'flaws' on the table, the other person will feel a certain way. You are not allowing them to truly see and get to know you, and to base their opinions off of who you are rather than the version of you that you want to portray. This can come from seeking a sense of control in the relationship and how you are perceived, usually to avoid possible rejection. This is ironic, because as long as we hold who we *really* are back from others, and can trust in the silences of a conversation, we will never be truly accepted as ourselves - we are avoiding intimacy and making rejection much more likely.

ADHD-ers may also tend to say yes automatically, without taking the time to think out whether they are actually able or willing to commit to something. This can result in unintentionally committing to plans you are unable to keep, or lying. White lies can pile on top of white lies when trying to cancel plans without making somebody 'feel bad'. It is very easy to unintentionally lie when speaking without thinking and to later realise your mistake, beat yourself up for it and reinforce the negative stories you may have about yourself.

As seen in 'H is for High-functioning', some ADHD-ers appear to be extremely well organised and put together. This 'busyness' can result in them missing out on life, as they rush from one social engagement to another, without having the time to properly slow down and focus on the person. They might appear distracted and uninterested in the person, who can feel like a second option. This is ironic as the person with ADHD feels that they are prioritising the person above themselves and they should be grateful, not annoyed! As seen in 'N is for No', people pleasing often backfires in this way - I have had to learn the hard way that relationships require quality over quantity.

We are also unlikely to be able to sustain levels of over-commitment for very long. As we saw in 'B is for Burnout', this can result in cancelling everything at short notice and not fulfilling promises because you have burned yourself out health-wise. Other people may feel that you are simply cancelling on them because you have better things to do!

This can cause serious problems if we happen to mix an impulsive idea of interest with a social connection. As seen in 'I is for Interests', it can be very hard for ADHD-ers to not make an interest their entire focus in life for a period of time. If this happens to involve work or other people in your life, such as starting a new business with friends, then this is usually something you do *not* want to rush into. Our infectious enthusiasm, quick minds and eagerness to to help others can result in us messily combining relationships and work, two very separate concepts.

The lack of boundaries between work and friends has caused me to lose many friendships over the years, due to a combination of burnout and losing interest. People who think things through a lot more thoroughly can understandably react badly when we lose interest in projects that mean a lot to them, after providing commitments in the past. We can also get inside our own heads and convince ourselves that we are only valued for what we are 'doing' for others, because we forge our social connections on these work-projects, and may over-extend ourselves, such as working for free.

This also ties in with the disorganised aspect of ADHD. Having a non-detail orientated mind, or one that is prone to hyper-focusing on certain things to the exclusion of all others, can mean that you easily forget appointments and commitments. As we will see in 'O is for Organisation', this can be tackled with a select few notebooks and planners, but it is highly possible that if you have ADHD, you have enough planners for every week of the year and to-do lists coming out of your ears. Having 18 to-do lists means that you are often unable to focus your mind on the things you do need to remember, which means that you can unintentionally stand people up or completely forget important dates, such as birthdays. This does not bode well for personal relationships!

Unsurprisingly, social anxiety is also sometimes seen in ADHD-ers. It can feel much easier to exclude yourself from the world than to have the pressures of socialising in polite society. I have felt a tremendous amount of anxiety around my family and friends as a result of my ADHD. I couldn't bear to explain to people what I had 'been up to' since the last time they saw me – it could involve anything from moving country to starting a new business and giving it all up!

When you set yourself up in a pattern of starting many projects and not being able to follow through on any of them, it can feel like everyone is waiting for you to fail, and you can project judgment where it doesn't exist. My life often felt like a soap opera that I was watching along with everybody else - and not in a good way.

It is incredibly hard to believe in yourself if you think that nobody else does either. As we saw in 'K is for Kindness', social connections are an extremely important aspect of being happy. You deserve to have good relationships with your friends and family, and to receive the love back that you provide to them.

How to have good relationships with your family and friends

1. Assess the people in your life. Put them into categories of 'unconditional love', 'close friends' and 'acquaintances'.

2. Assess how these people make you feel. Do they make you feel good or bad about yourself? Why are they in your life?

3. Consider each relationship in turn and decide how equal it is on a scale of 1 to 10, thinking about the things that you do for each other and the benefits you both enjoy from the relationship.

4. Identify if you want to continue the relationship, and if so, ways that you can make these relationships more equal. For example, could you ask a friend to help you with a particularly difficult task?

5. Write out ten boundaries for your relationships. These could include not mixing work with these people, not loaning money to or from them, thinking before saying yes to something, asking for help, not paying for other people and so on.

Other activities you can do to improve your relationships with your family and friends include:

- ❑ Write a letter to the people in your life that you want to improve your relationships with, acknowledging the impact that the relationship has in your life and thanking the person for being there. Be careful not to over-apologise for things you haven't done – we can often place a lot of unnecessary blame on ourselves.

- ❑ Read 'N is for No' to stop people pleasing. Only say what you mean, and mean what you say. Don't commit to things mindlessly or because you feel like you should.

- ❑ Notice how much effort other people put in to your relationships when you stop. This should be a good indicator of what you mean to them. For example, does someone only get in touch with you when they want something?

- ❑ Make an effort to really listen to people when they talk and maintain eye contact. A good way of doing this is repeating each word they say in your head, instead of trying to think of what to say in response.

- ❏ Ensure that you have a period of free time for yourself each week, even just half an hour. Make sure that your own battery is charged before giving energy to others, as in 'K is for Kindness'.

- ❏ Speak to people that you trust about ADHD and the way it affects you. Having an open, honest conversation about ADHD, even if you haven't been officially diagnosed, is a great way to explain the way that you can behave to other people in your life.

is for medication

Did you know?

- In the UK, healthcare providers should ensure that people with ADHD have a 'comprehensive, holistic shared treatment plan that addresses psychological, behavioural and occupational or educational needs' (National Institute for Health and Care Excellence, 2019). This demonstrates that medication by itself is not enough to treat ADHD - there should also be lifestyle adaptions where necessary.

- ADHD stimulant medication has been proven to be very effective, with a responsiveness rate of 70-80% (Biederman & Wilens et al, 2005). Stimulant medication helps to make the neurotransmitters in the ADHD brain that are not working so well to work functionally.

- A range of non-pharmacological solutions have been linked with positive effects on ADHD symptoms, including therapy, fish oil, exercise and getting enough sleep. Though the condition may change over time, it's with us for life, as ADHD cannot be outgrown.

Medication can be very tricky for people who have ADHD. For forgetful, impulsive people, even turning up to a doctor's appointment can be difficult enough – let alone go through the period of testing out medication to observe how your body reacts, remembering to take it each day and to organise your prescriptions each month.

Despite this frustration, ADHD medication can be life changing. The first time I took it, it felt like putting on glasses, having not been able to see for my entire life. I could suddenly see dust all over my flat, and the 500 thoughts that usually were competing for my attention at any one time had disappeared. I could actually listen to someone and focus on what they were saying, felt stronger in my body and easily do the things I usually avoided.

However, it has not been easy. The initial elation quickly wears off as it becomes 'normal', which is exactly how ADHD medication should make you feel - calm. It stimulates the neurotransmitters in your brain responsible for calming it down, which is why people who have ADHD have been known to self-medicate with alcohol, drugs, coffee or other stimulant increasing activities. I used to drink ten coffees per day pre-diagnosis, with virtually no side effects. In contrast, even one coffee has a huge effect on me when I have taken my medication now.

The medication can have also serious side effects. When I took too high of a dose, I lost 12 kilograms of weight in a month and suffered panic attacks on an almost daily basis. I was shaky, my mouth was always dry and I couldn't sleep. The private psychiatrist wanted to give me extra anti-anxiety medication, as we saw in 'D is for Diagnosis', instead of reducing the dose. I knew there was something not right in my body and refused to take more medication instead of less.

Finding the right dose is extremely important and it takes time. Taking ADHD medication is a huge decision for a number of reasons – not only will it have a hopefully positive, but possibly negative effect on your life, everybody seems to have an opinion on it as there is a lot of associated stigma. I had people around me telling me I shouldn't be 'taking speed' and saying that doctors were just prescribing this medication to make money. As a result, I felt embarrassed and unsure about taking it, especially because the side-effects were initially so strong, so I started only taking tablets on the days when I felt that I needed to concentrate - which resulted in an energy rollercoaster from hell. This type of self-medicating is extremely dangerous because it is going against medical advice and how the medication is supposed to work, which meant my body couldn't regulate itself properly.

Not only is the medication highly addictive, it is also EXPENSIVE. Privately, my prescription costs around £100 per month. I managed to get my prescription transferred to the NHS, which is part of the reasoning behind this book – if you are on a private prescription in the UK, I really recommend transferring to the NHS, which is very much possible. My private psychiatrist tried to put me off doing so with stories about waiting times to be diagnosed through the NHS, however, it was perfectly easy when I insisted on it.

My GP was able to continue the prescription whilst waiting for the official diagnosis through these channels, but it's good to check this with them before. The thought of not trusting what the psychiatrist was telling me seemed overwhelming, because if he was misleading me about the cost and NHS, then it was possible he had completely misdiagnosed me also and was just trying to get money out of me, as others had suggested. The thought of going through all of the diagnosis process again, once I had finally come around to accepting that I may have ADHD, was terrifying. It can feel extremely lonely and confusing, as you don't know who to trust - and if you can't trust the super expensive medical professionals, who can you trust?

Yourself. You are ultimately the only person that you can trust when it comes to understanding your own body and what you need. It was only when I became extremely unwell from the medication that I decided to take matters into my own hands and tell the psychiatrist I was no longer going to see him and wanted a referral letter written to my GP. Through the NHS, I took a break from medication and then started on the lowest dose, which helped me enormously.

Do not take one person's opinion as the final word, even if they are highly qualified and charging you a lot of money. There is no physical test to do to take ADHD, and people are misdiagnosed with medical conditions all the time. Doctors are also not immune to the stigma that surrounds ADHD, so if you don't agree with what you've been told by one, get a second opinion. In a 2017 survey, 22% of patients, and parents and caregivers of children with ADHD noted that their GP had expressed doubt about whether ADHD is real. (Born to Be ADHD, 2017)

ADHD stimulant medication also tends to be highly regulated as a 'controlled drug', which means in the UK, that doctors will not prescribe you more than one month's worth at a time. This can be a helpful metaphorical 'anchor', as in 'G is for Grounding', but difficult if you have trouble with organisation, routines and attending appointments – such as if you have ADHD! It is also important that your doctor properly monitors your use of the medication, taking your weight and blood pressure regularly, because the side effects can be dangerous. Now I see my doctor every 3 months for a check-up and call every month for a repeat prescription, which is sent directly to the pharmacy. It has taken a lot of refinement to get to this point, and was overwhelming at first, but it's just a matter of explaining your situation and asking for help when needed.

It can be scary to start taking ADHD medication for several reasons. I felt like this would make me weak, and was terrified of becoming dependent on the medication. I felt like I had started a life sentence, where I would have to pay hundreds of pounds for medication every month for the rest of my life, and ashamed of having to do this just to be 'normal'.

Having taken the right dose of medication consistently for over a year, I can say with absolute certainty that it has changed my life for the better. Nowadays I don't mention it to anyone in my life, and just treat it like a daily vitamin.

I worked through my fears by prioritising my own health above the opinions of others, which I still have to do every so often. It can feel as though I am 'cheating' somehow, by taking medication, and I have to remind myself that taking it just means that my brain is able to operate like everybody else's. My understanding is that if a person without ADHD took my medication, they would be bouncing off the walls - but for me, it just means that I can motivate myself to exercise *and* turn up to work on time in the morning.

The way to deal with medication-related anxiety is to be compassionate and kind to yourself, as in 'K is for Kindness'. We do not shame people for taking cancer medication. If you had a broken arm, you would use the sling. You would do whatever you could to get better as quickly as possible. If your partner had heart disease, you would be making sure they take that medication every single day. Yet, with mental health, it is often another story – because it is invisible, we don't treat it in the same way. Taking medication does not make you weak, it quite literally makes you stronger. Having ADHD is nothing to be ashamed about, as in 'W is for Weaknesses'.

ADHD Medication

At the time of writing, there are five types of medication licensed for the treatment of ADHD in the UK: methylphenidate, dexamfetamine, lisdexamfetamine, atomoxetine and guanfacine. They are not a cure for ADHD, but they help to reduce the negative symptoms. ADHD manifests differently in everybody and there is no one 'cure all' tablet - different medication will work for different people, and you might need to try a few to find the one that is right for you.

Side effects of these medication types can include:

- ❏ A decreased appetite – which means that you will have to force yourself to eat properly (3 meals a day!). It's important to be cautious of the medication if you have or have had disordered eating, as it can cause significant weight loss.

- ❏ Trouble sleeping – depending on the medication, you might experience a 'crash' when the effects wear off, meaning that you are more tired than usual. If you are taking too high of a dose, you might find it difficult to fall asleep at night.

- ❏ Headaches or stomachaches – these went away after a while for me, but I would advise drinking a lot of water and eating properly.

- ❏ Mood swings / anxiety – see 'Z is for Zen'. When I was taking too high of a dose, I had terrible anxiety and panic attacks, which can be a sign that the medication is not quite right for you.

- ❏ Dizziness, nausea, vomiting and diarrhea – in my experience, these become more likely if you don't follow the instructions of the medication, such as avoiding caffiene and alcohol.

- ❏ A dry mouth - my mouth was *so* dry at the start, but this went away after a few weeks.

- ❏ Skin problems - when I was on too high of a dose, I had terrible acne that I had never had before. This could be a sign of imbalances in your body.

It is extremely important that you speak to your doctor as soon as possible if you feel depressed, concerned, or do not experience the expected side effects. This is particularly vital in the first few days of taking the medication – if something doesn't feel right, tell someone you trust as soon as possible and stop taking it. Trust yourself and check in with your body regularly, as in 'Y is for Your Body'.

As this I am not a medical professional, this book will not go into the pros and cons of different types of ADHD medication. What I will say is please do try the medication that your doctor suggests. Don't be put off by the same fears as I was, and please don't try to outsmart the medical professionals by taking your own made up dose.

<u>Tips</u>

- ❏ Set yourself reminders to take your tablets at the right times each day - for example, by setting alarms on your phone.

- ❏ Try to establish a routine in taking your tablets so that it becomes an automatic part of your day, as in 'G is for

Grounding'. For example, I keep my medication in a box next to my bed and take it as soon as I wake up in the morning.

- ❑ Try to incorporate a way of knowing whether you have take your medication or not, for example, using boxes with days of the week on them, or ticking off a list when taking the pill.
- ❑ If you find the medication is not working for you or there is a problem with it, speak to your doctor as soon as possible.
- ❑ Avoid telling people who do not necessarily need to know that you are taking medication, but do make sure that you speak to someone you trust about it. It is helpful to have a second opinion of how the medication may affect you.
- ❑ Only take the medication that is prescribed and read the instructions!
- ❑ Don't skip tablets. Trust the doctor and take them every day as prescribed without overthinking it. Give yourself at least a year of taking them before thinking about whether you should stop.
- ❑ Do trust your gut and speak to people if something doesn't feel quite right, such as if you are having continued negative side effects.
- ❑ Make sure that you eat properly and drink plenty of water. Ask someone to help you with this if you can. Look at the diet section below and try to ensure you eat three meals a day no matter what.

- ❏ Try to avoid energy-spiking stimulants whilst on ADHD medication, such as coffee. They tend to not react very well together and you don't need any more energy!

- ❏ NEVER give anyone else your medication to take. ADHD medication affects people differently and can be incredibly dangerous for someone else to take.

- ❏ Have an pill in a designated wallet on you at all times or somewhere where you can easily access it, such as at work. This is your emergency pill in case you forget to take one - but don't worry too much if you do forget to take one! The advice I have received is just to take one the day next day as normal, whilst understanding that you might be a bit tired and emotional during the non-medicated day.

- ❏ If you take more than one tablet accidentally, do not worry, but try to speak to a doctor as soon as possible. I did this once and just had to have sick day from work, where I very energetically cleaned my flat for many hours! You may feel all of the associated side-effects very strongly, such as headaches and having a dry mouth.

- ❏ Speak to your doctor about how you can renew your prescription each month and what might work best for you. Set a calendar reminder for at least 5 days before your medication runs out, so you can follow up on this - you could also ask your pharmacist to give you a telephone call as a reminder.

Some people may not be able to take traditional ADHD medication for medical reasons, or if they are pregnant. How

I try to see the medication is as something that I take at the moment to help me build up the scaffolding discussed in 'G is for Grounding'. I am training myself to live a life where I will hopefully not need to take medication in the future, because all of the routines I need to stay in control of my ADHD will be in place. So although medication can be incredibly helpful, it is not *vital* to thriving without ADHD. You can train yourself in other ways – which is the reason for this book!

Therapy

Therapy is really important for someone with ADHD. Though you might find that you talk continuously for 50 minutes, it is an incredible activity to just be able to be completely yourself without having to think about anyone else and metaphorically empty your brain.

It is important to find the right therapist for you, however, and I respond better to those who are pro-active and have an understanding of ADHD. Therapy can be expensive and difficult to stick to if you aren't feeling that it is immediately helpful - and the job of most therapists is just to listen. I eventually found a therapist who understood that I might dip in and out of sessions as needed, instead of sticking to a weekly schedule, and who was able to give me advice, which I found really helpful.

Cognitive behavioural therapy is a useful method of providing you with the skills to change how you think and behave – kind of similar to the exercises throughout this book. Therapy may be available through the healthcare system in your country, but there are often waiting lists.

As ADHD-ers may be searching for someone to help them proactively change their habits, get things done and hold them accountable, coaches can be really helpful. This is especially so if they are specialised in ADHD - I started seeing an ADHD coach who has been so incredibly helpful, as they understand the specific issues that I encounter and how to best motivate and support me.[8] There are also coaching communities, such as ADHD Unlocked, which can be hugely beneficial and cost-effective in terms of having a support network and being able to speak to people who are having the same experiences.

There may be Government support schemes which can help with funding for job coaches related to your ADHD, as in 'J is for Jobs', or therapy available from the NHS. It's a good idea to research the different options available and to always check whether a professional has experience with ADHD.

Diet

The food that we put into our bodies have an enormous effect on our minds. For minds that are searching for stimulation, sugar, caffeine and alcohol can easily hit the sweet spot. The problem with this is that these energy highs are short lived, addictive and terrible for our bodies. I used to live on chocolate bars and coffee, which caused me to be exhausted and weak. Sugary drinks can seem like an instant hit of energy and focus, but the effect quickly wears off to leave us depleted and tired.

For ADHD-ers, cooking can seem a bit long winded and boring. I used to be terrible at following recipes, and would just throw in a rough guess of the measurements required.

---
[8] https://www.theadhdadvocate.com/

This usually ended up in slightly weird tasting food and a messy kitchen that I would be unable to muster up the energy to clean. Eating take out and food grabbed on the go was much easier.

However in the same way, this 'fast food' gives us short energy spikes, followed by exhaustion. ADHD-ers can often suffer with sleep problems, as seen in 'S is for Sleep', and having a diet of sugar and caffeine only makes these problems worse. It is also not great for our spending to be in the habit of buying coffee or lunch every day, which can quickly add up, as seen in 'F is for Finances'.

Learning to cook is one of the best things you can do for yourself. Incorporating cooking and proper time to eat meals into your routine, as in 'G is for Grounding', will change your life and allow you to be in control of your energy instead of being at the mercy of sugar and caffeine.

It is a good idea to try and eliminate as much sugar, coffee, alcohol and fast food as you can from your diet. Make an assessment of what you would typically eat in a week and think about how you feel as a result. Identify what your triggers are for eating certain types of food (for example, I binge eat chocolate when I am feeling stressed) and what your blocks are for not eating healthily (for example, not having the time to cook breakfast).

Assess how your diet can become healthier and the things that you can do to overcome your blocks. For example, if you don't have the time to make breakfast, make it the night before! If you usually grab something on your lunch break, make the effort to take in lunch.

Tips

- ❑ Invest in a slow cooker. This is my saviour in the kitchen – just throw the ingredients in, leave it for a few hours and come home to food!
- ❑ Cook one big meal each weekend that you can eat the entire week without thinking about it.
- ❑ If you get stressed thinking about what to cook, eat the same meals every day. Plan them out on the weekend and make it part of your routine.
- ❑ Clean your kitchen as you cook, playing your favourite music.
- ❑ If you struggle with buying ingredients, invest in a food delivery service. I use Oddbox, which deliver cheap boxes of fruit and vegetables that have been saved from being thrown away due to not being the perfect shapes for sale.
- ❑ Ask somebody to teach you how to cook. My best friend taught me the basics and is very happy now that I can cook for her!
- ❑ Incorporate taking vitamin supplements into your routine. Fish oil, omega 3 fatty acids and zinc have been suggested to help with ADHD symptoms.

Exercise

As in 'E is for Exercise', exercise increases the production of dopamine and endorphins in your body, which have a similar effect on the brain as taking ADHD medication. The difference is that the effects may only last for a few hours, instead of the whole day.

I would hugely recommend incorporating exercise into your daily routine any way that you can, even if it is just walking to work instead of getting public transport, or having a stretch before bed. It will clear your mind and burn off any excess energy you might have, allowing you to focus better throughout the day and sleep well at night.

Mindfulness

Mindfulness is a great way to train your brain how *you* want to, and some forms, such as 'meditative mindfulness' have also been proven to have a positive effect on ADHD symptoms (Mitchell JT, McIntyre EM, English JS, et al., 2017). This refers to being in the present moment and consciously choosing your thoughts instead of allowing them to infiltrate your mind at all times. Slowing down and being present can be very difficult for an ADHD-er, but there are ways of hacking mindfulness to work for you, as in 'Z is for Zen'.

Being kind to yourself, as in 'K is for Kindness', is another very important factor in improving your ADHD. Being kind to ourselves allows us to reason with our own minds to change our negative behaviours, because this will result in the best scenario for us. When we fundamentally care about ourselves, we will want to make sure that we eat proper food, or live in a clean environment, or stay in a stable job. When we recognise that we deserve to be happy, we can turn our attention to figuring out the best way of finding and keeping that happiness.

is for no

Did you know?

- Many people with ADHD suffer from emotional dysregulation, hyper-sensitivity to rejection and low self-esteem. ADHD-ers may struggle with saying 'no', or thinking things through properly before saying yes, in order to please others. As in 'Y is for Your Body', sensory issues can accompany ADHD which can contribute to us not being able to understand our own needs on even the most basic levels - which then can't be communicated to others!

- ADHD has been linked to problems in processing communication, resulting in misunderstandings with others. For example, zoning out during a conversation, or having memory problems causing them to forget what they have previously said. This can result in shame and 'white lies' in an attempt to fix the situation, often manifesting as people pleasing (Bernstein, 2010).

- The Rejection Sensitive Dysphoria that is said to accompany ADHD can result in people with ADHD becoming people pleasers. Dr William Dodson said people with RSD 'quickly scan every person they meet and have a remarkable ability to figure out exactly what that person would admire or praise… they are so intent on avoiding the possibility of displeasure from others and keeping everyone happy that they often lose track of their own desires' (Dodson, Emotional Regulation and Rejection Sensitivity, 2016).

Having a quick mind that tends to act before thinking things through properly means that ADHD-ers can be prone to committing to things that they might not actually want to do, and saying things that they don't mean. Combined with other ADHD symptoms such as having a short attention span and being hyper-sensitive to possible rejection, this can mean that we feel desperate for the acceptance and love of other people and will do anything to get it.

This results in people pleasing. People pleasing is putting other people before yourself, acting out of 'feeling bad' or wanting to be 'nice'. It often comes from a place of searching for acceptance and expectations, resulting in very unequal relationships. It can feel like subconsciously choosing to exploit yourself for others in the hope that they will like you.

The irony in this is that people rarely react the way that you want them to, despite your best efforts. Nobody can control how another person feels. Some people are not going to like you and that is the end of it – there isn't any amount of flowers, notes or kindness that you can give them to change their minds. Another irony of people pleasing is that you often actually end up pleasing nobody at all, because you are so exhausted from spreading yourself so thinly that you actually can't fully commit to anything or anyone, as in 'B is for Burnout'.

You may also tend to prioritise people that are more 'toxic' and prone to exploiting this over those who truly care and want the best for you. The latter group will be the ones who will understand when you cancel, who will try to be there for you when you need them. The former are the ones who will get angry when you don't match their expectations, the ones who explicitly ask things of you and understand how to manipulate your emotions to suit them.

People pleasing can often result in sabotaging relationships simply by wanting to be liked. It can make a relationship uneven and result in you putting certain people in your life on pedestals – often seen in dating, as in 'X is for X-rated' – which are impossible for them to live up to. The person you put on a pedestal may not ask for you to do the things that you do for them, might feel bad that they aren't showing the same effort back to you or be slightly suspicious about your motives. They can feel under pressure themselves to appease your people pleasing and to show 'enough' gratitude as a result. You can also set yourself impossible standards to live up to and sustain in the long term.

Another way that people pleasing can affect your relationships is by lying. We might try to get out of tricky situations with a white lie or an excuse, because we feel too 'bad' saying the truth - such as we simply don't want to see someone. These lies can be hard to keep track of and can often easily be found out. This can also manifest as overpromising or setting impossible expectations on ourselves that we cannot meet, perpetuating feelings of insecurity and guilt.

It can also result in oversharing personal information which can make another person feel uncomfortable, when the intention is to fill the silences in a conversation. People pleasing is ultimately down to a lack of proper boundaries and not feeling able to trust that the other person will like you even if you aren't 'doing' things for them.

'K is for Kindness' shows the errors in this way of thinking - you are worthy of being liked just as you are. You also do not need to be liked by everyone - do you like everyone you meet? These are the questions we need to ask ourselves - do we even like the person ourselves? Often, we are running on such autopilot modes that it can be difficult to even stop and consider the possibility of not liking another person, or prioritising our own needs first.

You don't need to have ADHD to be prone to people pleasing. It has become embedded into our society, which values 'busyness' over having time to relax, and being a 'good' person, employee, friend, family member and so on... essentially, being able to do it all. These unrealistic expectations are perpetuated to us through social media, where we are reachable 24 hours, 7 days a week. You are simply a human being at the end of the day, and only have a limited capacity in how much you can do - and your first priority needs to be yourself. By valuing yourself, you will be guided as to what and who else you should be valuing in your life, instead of automatically accepting everything.

Checking in with yourself

To stop people pleasing, you have to focus on training your brain to make space between the time that somebody makes a request of you and your answer – or the time between your thinking of offering help to another person and actually offering it. That is all. In this space, your job is to think about whether you actually want to do the activity. Not whether you want the positive feeling of someone seemingly appreciating your generosity, but whether you literally, physically want to do the activity. This is called checking in with yourself.

This involves weighing up the pros and cons, and thinking of other considerations. Do you have the *time* to do this activity? What will it be costing you – the 'opportunity cost' of doing this activity? If is accepting a dinner invitation on a Thursday night for example, does this mean that you will be exhausted on Friday? What are all of the potential costs – how much could this dinner cost you in terms of money? Can you afford it? Try to feel your body for any signs of resistance – is your neck tensing up as you imagine going out for dinner with this person that you aren't sure if you like?

If you want to take it the extra mile, try to think about how this could potentially affect you in the future. For example, will accepting a dinner invitation make you feel obligated to this person? Would you feel anxiety at the thought of the bill coming and having to offer to split it? Would you drink alcohol and potentially regret it?

Try to think of the alternatives to the activity, just to consider them as options. Could you go for a coffee with this person in the day time instead? Could you arrange to spend time together when you have don't have to worry about working the next day?

Finally, consider saying no. What is the worst-case scenario of saying no? I used to act out of 'feeling bad' for people all of the time, because I was terrified to say no. 'No' teaches people to respect your boundaries. If you say no to somebody, the world is not going to end. If they are entitled to say no, you are too. Boundaries help us to respect ourselves and other people.

Then make a decision. The idea is to ultimately make this process automatic so that you don't have to think about it so much.

A great way to train yourself into checking in with yourself is by literally delaying your answer. Make sure that you do not say yes with the intention of changing this later, but simply say, 'can I let you know the answer to this later? I need to check my schedule.' Try to do this for an entire day and see what happens. I find it helpful to have a general stance of always sleeping on any big decisions - things tend to look different the next day!

Prioritising yourself

This is something that may not come naturally to people who can be more occupied with the opinions of others than their own. However, it is vitally important to start taking responsibility for your own happiness and letting others be responsible for theirs. No one is going to treat you exactly how you treat them and the only feelings you can control are your own.

To prioritise yourself, follow the below steps:

1. Write out a list of your <u>needs</u> in the following areas:

    - ❑ **Sleep** (how many hours do you need a night to feel rested? Is this ever interrupted by people pleasing – such as loud housemates or talking to someone late at night?)

    - ❑ **Eating** (what kind of food you want to eat and how you can eat it – do you need to use the kitchen, for example?)

    - ❑ **Mindfulness** (how often do you relax and have uninterrupted time to do 'nothing'?)

    - ❑ **Health** (how much alcohol / drugs do you consume? What do you need to do to avoid getting sick? What makes you feel healthy? How are you exercising your body?)

- ❑ **Home** (what do you need from your living environment? Are you a clean or messy person?)
- ❑ **Finances** (how much money do you need to survive? What do you need to prioritise in terms of spending? How much do you spend on yourself?)
- ❑ **Social life** (how much interaction with friends and family do you need to feel connected?)
- ❑ **Dating** (what do you need in a relationship to feel secure and happy?)
- ❑ **Hobbies** (what hobbies do you need to do to make you happy? How often?)
- ❑ **Physical appearance** (what do you need to do to feel good about how you look?)
- ❑ **Work** (what do you need from your job? Are you doing anyone else's job, or taking on too much at work?)

2. Now assess the areas listed above and identify how you please others. Make a list of all the ways that you people please and have done in the past. What have been the worst things that have happened to you as a result of your people pleasing?

3. Write out a list of 3 experiences of people pleasing that have left you feeling angry. Try to look at the experiences from the perspective of the other person and write out how they may have felt from a calm point of view.

4. Make a list of boundaries based on your needs identified earlier as present form statements. For example:

   ❏ I do not commit myself to relationships that I do not want to be in

   ❏ I do not work past 6pm

   ❏ I do not pay for other people's meals

   ❏ I am allowed to take up space in my own house

   ❏ I tell people when their behaviour negatively affects my needs

5. Identify ways that you can enforce these boundaries and overcome any triggers to them. For example, committing yourself to 'checking in' with yourself every time someone asks something of you, so setting a time delay on answering any requests.

6. Be aware of people who try to infiltrate your boundaries. When we initially set a boundary, this can feel like we have 'ticked the box' and then we give in to persistence from the other person. This would be likely from a person who benefits from your people pleasing and understands how to make you feel guilty. Refuse to have 'porous boundaries' – you have done the work of setting it out, so don't let someone squeeze through the gaps! If you find that this happens, don't be afraid to restate your boundaries and stand up for yourself.

7. Following on from this, notice who tries to make you feel bad for standing up for yourself and who is upset at your new boundaries. See chapter 'L is for Love' and

think about whether this person is deserving of being in your life at all if they do not respect you. Don't be afraid to cut out toxic people!

Practicing saying no

Saying no used to bring about terrible feelings of guilt and anxiety for me. I would happily prefer to be humiliated than stand up for myself in an awkward situation and to be seen as 'difficult'. I felt like I needed to have a justifiable 'reason' to say no, such as saying that I was in a relationship if a stranger asked me on a date, rather than being able to simply say no. Especially for women, our society teaches us to be 'polite' and accommodating, and we can internalise messaging that saying no is rude and offensive.

No is a complete sentence. It is not rude or offensive to not want to do something.

As a result of our conditioning, it can be very useful to figure out the practicalities of saying no.

1. Think of the times you have said no in the past. Why have you said no – what are your core values underlying these? How about times that you have said yes when you wanted to say no – what stopped you?

2. Write a list of ways that you could have said no in the latter situations and practice saying them out loud in the mirror. Try to avoid including excuses or any situations in which you as yes at first and plan to change your mind later – this is always much harder to do!

3. Think of situations in the future that could arise where you may be prone to people pleasing. Apply a statement for each of these situations – for example, if you have a party coming up that you may want to leave early this could be, 'thank you so much for a great night. I have to go home now'. Remember that you don't need to give a reason or excuse, and that you do not owe anyone any justifications for how you feel.

4. Intentionally put yourself in an awkward but safe situation where you can practice saying no. For example, pay for something small with a £20 note and do not apologise to the cashier. If they ask if you have any smaller change, say 'no I don't'. People pleasing can often manifest as repeated apologies for things we have no need to apologise for, putting the other person above us.

5. Afterwards, notice the way that you feel and how the situation played out differently to how you may have imagined it would. The world is still spinning and everyone is still alive. Recognise how the person's responsibility for how they feel belongs to them – list the reasons that you were well within your means to say no in this situation. For example, it is a cashier's job to provide you with change. You are not obligated to have the exact amount of money. You are purchasing something from them and are in an equal relationship.

6. Remember to watch out for people who try to make you feel bad about stating your boundary and to uphold it no matter what. Don't allow other people to tell you how to feel.

Stop apologising

If you are prone to people pleasing, you might find yourself apologising incessantly. Has anyone ever knocked into you on the street and you have found yourself apologising to them? Saying 'sorry' has become a part of our culture, simply apologising for taking up space and having needs.

Apologising for things that you don't have to be sorry for means that you are in a constant state of guilt and feeling bad about yourself, automatically rewriting situations to make yourself the guilty party, putting the other person above you. See 'K is for Kindness' if this resonates with you! I used to feel terrible about tiny things all the time, not realising that people literally *do not care that much*. They are resilient human beings, just as you are, and it is quite literally impossible to know how they feel. People may feel ways for reasons that have nothing to do with you, and it is pointless to spend time worrying about whether somebody likes you or not.

Saying sorry for things you do not bear responsibility for can be a way of trying to gain control in a situation, but it tends to backfire when you are constantly beating yourself up and putting yourself down. People around you can also become frustrated at your apologies, as it makes the times when you should take responsibility and apologise for something less meaningful. Apologies have a lot of value in mending conflict, which every relationship will experience at one point or another, no matter how hard we to try to avoid it.

The key with this is to notice every time that you apologise. Write it down on your phone or ask your friend to call you out every time that you say 'sorry'. You might be surprised at how many times you say it in a day. Each time it happens, notice why you said it and who's responsibility this actually is. Don't apologise for saying sorry!

O

is for organisation

Did you know?

- ADHD can cause serious issues with organisation, as this is what our pre-frontal cortex is responsible for, which is unregulated for ADHD-ers. There may also be sensory issues, as in 'Y is for Your Body', which can make us oblivious towards 'mess'.

- Particularly when ADHD is undiagnosed and untreated, it has been said to contribute to problems succeeding in school and successfully graduating, at work, lost productivity and reduced earning power, more accidents whilst driving and problems with the law (ADHD Awareness Month, 2020).

- A 2017 survey of 800 teachers found that 55% reported concerns about possible undiagnosed ADHD in their students. 74% of these teachers did not know that learners with ADHD have difficulties in organisation and planning (Comres, 2017).

Organisation utilises our executive functioning skills, which ADHD-ers can struggle with. The part of the brain that is responsible for making decisions, memory and detail is affected by ADHD (the pre-frontal cortex), which can make everything seem like organised chaos. Ironically, some people with ADHD may appear extremely organised, such as those in 'H is for High-functioning', because of finding coping mechanisms throughout their life to help them manage this. Others may be the complete opposite!

Focusing your mind

Having ADHD can mean that your mind can feel quite jumbled up. Dates, times, details and facts can all become a mishmash as attention rapidly changes from one thing to the next. This can become extremely frustrating for ADHD-ers and those around them, and result in anxiety trying to communicate the chaos inside your mind to the outside world.

Everybody is different, but for me writing things out really helps. This is particularly beneficial in terms of work and having meetings, as I tend to panic when put on the spot. Writing out what I want to say before every meeting and taking it with me helps me to neatly summarise what I want to communicate and ironically, appear very organised!

Mindfulness and meditation can also be very helpful in terms of relaxing your mind to try and focus on one thing. If you have ADHD, you may find yourself overusing your brain in certain areas and underusing it in others, so it is good to try and balance out the energy across all of the mind. If you imagine your brain as a television with all 15 channels playing at once, it can feel virtually impossible to concentrate on only one of them – however you *can* train your brain to do so. It requires sustained mental effort and practice, but this is nature's remedy to overthinking. You just need to give your brain a rest.

Help yourself out in doing this as much as possible by cutting out any unnecessary distractions. Focusing with ADHD can sometimes feel like you are trying to work on a computer with 20 tabs open, in a room with music playing loudly out of surround sound speakers, your phone flashing with notifications beside you, the television blaring and with a small herd of animals and children continuously running through the door. The great news is that you can literally and metaphorically remove the unnecessary tabs, turn off the music and television, put your phone on aeroplane mode and lock the door.

Part of this is recognising the distractions that are there. Think about what you find yourself doing when you procrastinate – do you spend hours on social media, clean up your house or call a friend? Virtually anything except what you are supposed to be doing? Try to think of ways that you can stop yourself from procrastinating. For example, if you are addicted to your phone, can you leave it at home when you go to work – or ask your colleague to put it in their drawer for the morning? More examples of anti-procrastination hacks can be found in 'P for Procrastination'.

Our phones and the internet are great for learning, but not so great for overloading our minds with unnecessary information that has no relevance to us. We are quite literally bombarded with constant information – whether that is what a stranger ate for breakfast or the news in a foreign country. It is a good idea to try and reduce the amount of information you expose your mind to in order to focus it on what matters most to you.

If you have ADHD, you might have 10 different to-do lists and journals (at least!), or none at all. The secret to organising your mind is to make it simple. This means as minimal lists as possible. Though they can be extremely helpful, having lists upon lists and piles of journals to keep track of will have the opposite effect in terms of productivity. The ideal scenario is one journal for 'home' and one for 'work'. The home journal should contain a list of all of your various administrative accounts and any to-do lists related to your personal life, diary entries, important dates to remember and so on. Make sure it is well hidden in your house, so that if someone broke in it would be very difficult for them to find!

The work journal should contain information you would be ok with a colleague seeing – to-do lists relating to work, for example. I find it very helpful to write a to-do list every morning so that my day is focused - even better to use is a whiteboard, so that you can be regularly reminded of your priorities in a visual way.

With to-do lists, a good technique is to only have three things on it at a time. If you can get a portable whiteboard, it's helpful to prioritise your day by dividing it into three sections: 'important but not urgent', 'urgent and important', 'not urgent and not important'. The 'urgent and important' things are your focus to get done first. The 'not urgent and not important' part you can fill with any thoughts that pop up throughout the day, that could otherwise be distracting. Even if you're not working, it can be helpful to plan your non-working days this way, as it can be difficult to know how to organise our free time.

When it come to the tasks themselves, it's good to separate each one into manageable chunks. The key is making every task as basic and manageable as possible, and giving yourself more time than you think you will need. We will discuss more about this in 'T is for Time Management', but it's a good idea to set yourself a timer for each task, and to take regular breaks.

Tips

- ❏ Reduce the number of distractions around you. Figure out what they are and how you can overcome them - see 'J is for Jobs' for more on this specific to working.

- ❏ Try to reduce the amount of time you spend on your phone. You can keep track of your screen time, charge it in a different room to the one that you sleep in or put it in a specific place throughout the day when focusing on other things.

- ❏ Have a routine each day that you can do on autopilot, for example, by eating the same breakfast each morning.

- ❏ Recognise when you have the most energy in the day and prioritise your focus according to this.

- ❏ Tackle the tasks that you least want to do first in the day - think of your willpower like a battery that recharges when you sleep!

- ❏ Set yourself a timer (25 minutes has been proven to be optimal) of focus time, with 5-minute break periods (University of Illinois at Urbana-Champaign, 2011). It's helpful to have a clock or stop-watch to do this, because using our phones can often lead to being distracted by other things!

- ❏ Prioritise tasks into 'urgent but not important', 'important but not urgent' and 'urgent and important'. Focus on the latter first, and break tasks down into separate steps of what you need to do.

- ❏ Give yourself longer than you think you will need.

- ❏ Set yourself one to-do list per day, focusing on three things at a time only. You could write these three things on a post-it note or whiteboard.

- ❏ Try the grounding techniques in 'G is for Grounding', such as meditation, to signal to your brain that it is time to focus.

- ❏ Ensure that your diet is healthy and balanced, and that you incorporate meal times and proper breaks into your day.

Improving your memory

Having ADHD can mean that you are focused on the bigger picture, rather than the details. Having a short attention span with an aversion to focusing on things we don't want to focus on can mean that ADHD-ers can find themselves constantly forgetting belongings, dates, appointments, names and so on.

This can place a strain on interpersonal relationships, as people can equate forgetfulness with rudeness or simply not caring about them – such as forgetting birthdays!

This can also be problematic in terms of work, as seen in 'J is for Jobs'. Our work may expect us to be able to remember our various passwords to different systems or remember the different sign off processes involved for different projects. Details are often very important when it comes to work – time is money. Spending hour trying to remember your password, being locked out of your account and having to see IT to get back in is an hour of work missed.

The good news is that it is possible to hack your memory. You can remind yourself of what you need to remember and prepare in advance.

Tips

- ❑ Did your parents ever tell you to 'pack your school bag the night before?' Apply this to your life – prepare for tomorrow, today. Think about what you need for the day and make sure you have everything that you might need in your bag, or that everything is done which you can do beforehand, such as making yourself lunch.

- ❑ Have a phone charger on you at all times, including one specifically for your workplace.

- ❑ Write yourself a list of the things you need to check before leaving the house, and stick it on the door. Make sure it is simple, short and attention-grabbing!

- ❑ Put a large keyring on your keys, such as a handkerchief.

- ❑ For things that you are at high risk of losing such as ID cards or glasses, hook them onto necklaces, chains or elastic bands. I have a hairband on my printer card and automatically pop it onto my wrist after using it instead of leaving it by the printer!

- ❑ Have a dedicated spot, such as a bowl, for your keys, wallet and anything else that you are prone to losing in your house. Make it an automatic part of your routine to place these items in their home so that you know where they are at all times.

- ❏ Set yourself calendar reminders on your phone or computer for appointments – the day before and the hour before! Make it a habit to check your calendar every day.

- ❏ Make an effort to listen to people when they talk. Maintain eye contact and focus on what they are saying rather than thinking about what to say next.

- ❏ Post yourself visual reminders of things to remember where you will see them, for example by using a whiteboard to write any reminders on.

- ❏ Give a spare set of keys to somebody you trust who lives nearby so that you never have to call the locksmith again!

- ❏ Have a chart to fill in when you have done something, or take a photograph on your phone, such as when taking your medication, so that you know that you have done it. I also used to clap my hands or say a specific word when locking my door, which reminded me that I had done it later on, so I didn't have to go back and check!

- ❏ Write all of your passwords and various account details in one journal which is easy for you to access, that is well-hidden in your house. Try to reduce the number of email accounts that you use to one, and do a 'subscription inventory', as in 'F is for Finance' - taking away all those that you do not need.

- ❏ When you are in control of deadlines, give yourself far more time than you need. When you are given a deadline, make a new, shorter deadline for yourself so that it feels more urgent. More on this can be seen in 'T is for Time Management'.

Organising your space

The chaos in the mind of a person with ADHD can sometimes find its way into their outside world... often resulting in a physical mess. Again, this is not only difficult for those with ADHD to find their belongings and feel a sense of calm, but also those around them who may be exposed to the mess also. For example, living in a share house can be problematic if one person has a different understanding of what mess is to the others.

Before taking my medication, I was oblivious to mess. I was focused on the overall tidiness at a glance – swooping all of the mess in the cupboard or underneath the bed, as opposed to the crumbs, hair and dust steadily piling up. I didn't understand the difference between folding a shirt into a general square shape and folding it properly.

Learning how to see the mess is the first step for organising your space. Making a cleaning routine allows you to keep on top of the mess that builds up over the course of a week, which is especially helpful if you live with others. Putting a cleaning routine somewhere you will see it, such as the fridge, along with reminders on your phone is helpful.

When you are cleaning, take the time to do it properly. Spend time focusing on the details, on cleaning all aspects of the room instead of the general middle. As in the previous section, break the task down into smaller chunks. Give yourself specific tasks to do, such as hoovering, and identify how you will do it, setting measurable and achievable goals. If you really struggle with this, consider hiring a cleaner to come in every month or so - it can save you a lot of time and contribute to being more productive in other areas instead!

Living in a messy environment can sometimes be a result of things building up that we don't need. As seen in 'F is for Finance', ADHD-ers can be prone to impulsive spending, which can result in the accumulation of lots of physical objects. Regular routines of sorting through your belongings to either sell or give away the things that you do not need are very helpful. A good test when you do this is to assess how often you have used the object – if it isn't within the last year, lose it. This can also be applied to more perishable goods, such as a weekly clean out of your fridge.

Tips

- ❏ Have a cleaning routine and stick to it. Ask somebody to help you identify what tasks need to be done in your living area and for any advice on cleaning products – they will likely be very happy to help!

- ❏ Invest in proper cleaning products to clean your space with, which will motivate you to do the job properly. Read the instructions of how to use and maintain these products, such as how to replace hoover bags.

- ❏ Build daily cleaning into your routine, as in 'G is for Grounding'. For example, set yourself 5 minutes per day to clean as much of your room as possible, or ensure that you make your bed every morning. Set yourself small, achievable goals to build into your daily life.

- ❏ Schedule regular clean outs and don't be afraid to get rid of the belongings that you don't use.

- ❏ Build 'homes' for your belongings. For example, paper trays for bits of paper, a key hook for your keys, a cutlery drawer and so on. If everything has its' own place, you will be able to return it easily.

- ❏ Make cleaning fun! Play your favourite music and dance around as you clean.

Organising your 'life administration'

As we saw in 'G is for Grounding', routine and structure are very important for managing ADHD symptoms. They are the framework off which you can live your life, the things that should be done on autopilot so that you can use your brain for the things you want to focus on instead of worrying about small things throughout the day.

When it comes to life admin, there are a few different concepts that ADHD-ers can struggle with. These tend to be in the form of paperwork, bills, tax returns, doctor's appointments and so on – anything that is a bit difficult to quickly wrap your head around. Leaving these things to the last minute, or avoiding them all together is a recipe for disaster. Not only do you spend a lot of time worrying about them, even on a subconscious level, but it also tends to always be more stressful and worse if you leave things until the last minute.

Establishing a routine for life admin will improve your life dramatically. Sorting out these things as they happen, rather than when you seriously *have* to, will result in far less stress. They can seem extremely overwhelming and therefore our brains tend to run away from them all together (perpetuating the cycle of not being 'normal' and able to cope with routine activities) but when we actually get down to it, can be quite straightforward. There are also people available to help you, even more so if you leave enough time to do them.

There are a few steps to getting on top of life admin:

1. Make a list of all of the life admin tasks that you know that you will need to acknowledge at some point in the next year. For example:

    - ❏ Tax return
    - ❏ Paying bills
    - ❏ Paying rent / mortgage payments
    - ❏ Doctor's check ups
    - ❏ Dentist check ups
    - ❏ Haircuts
    - ❏ Eye tests

2. Put a date next to each task that you have identified. Dedicate one hour to arranging all of the appointments you have identified. Now set yourself calendar reminders – for a month, week and day before, and on the day itself.

3. Take the time to set up a direct debit for the bills that need paying. Dedicate some time to figuring out how much each bill costs you and a budget, as in 'F is for Finance'.

4. Make a system for tackling life admin as soon as it arises. For example, when you receive a letter, put it in a specific place, such as a letter holder on your table.

Dedicate a certain amount of time each weekend to life admin and going through these tasks that minute instead of putting them off any longer.

5. If the process of dealing with the life admin becomes stressful and overwhelming (such as being put on hold for a long period of time), engage in a mindfulness break as in 'Z is for Zen'. Don't be afraid to ask for help from the people around you – these things are tricky for everyone!

6. When you need to focus, consider asking a friend if they want to do a 'focus session' with you. You can either sit together on do this remotely, but dedicate a set amount of time to completing one of these tasks where you both can hold each other accountable - it is very effective! There are also online ways of doing this, such as Focusmate, which will connect you with a virtual co-worker.

is for procrastination

Did you know?

- It can be very difficult to concentrate on and finish tasks for people with ADHD, who are very prone to distraction and procrastination.

- Research published in 2018 found that 75% of individuals with ADHD were classified as 'chronic procrastinators', confirming that procrastination is a pervasive issue for ADHD-ers. (Taylor, 2018)

- As in 'T is for Time Management', ADHD causes impairments in relation to our sense of time - so organisational problems could be addressed by externally stimulating our brains when a project needs completing.

The short attention span and impacted executive functioning associated with ADHD can contribute to issues with self-motivation. This underlies the overwhelming feeling at the thought of filling out a form, making an appointment or following a process. Our brains like to skip straight to the finish line, as quickly as possible – or not at all. We tend to encounter many distractions along the way that lead us to procrastinate - where we delay or postpone actions that need doing.

Whilst it might be very easy for a person with ADHD to set up a company overnight, it could be virtually impossible for them to do their washing. This is incredibly frustrating as we understand that we *have* the energy – we just don't seem to be able to choose what we focus our attention on. This is what leads to the stigma of ADHD-ers being defined as 'lazy', perpetuating the cycle of insecurity and self-hate, as in 'K is for Kindness'.

When our mind is not wanting to focus on the thing we are trying to do, we are prone to procrastination - being distracted. It can feel like somebody else has the television remote to your focus, changing channels despite us our best trying to focus on one thing.

I find myself procrastinating by endlessly scrolling through social media, cleaning, talking to friends, watching television, writing – anything except what I am supposed to be doing. Focusing our mind takes up an intense amount of mental energy, as seen in 'O is for Organisation', and can exhaust us.

There are many ways that you can train yourself to stop procrastinating and start focusing.

Control your use of social media

Social media is designed to be addictive. It is a procrastination paradise, filled with lots of short, surface level content that is novel and fun - which has *literally been designed to distract us* - to grab and keep our attention, a valuable commodity. The issue is that we are often not actively choosing to spend our attention in this way, but rather become distracted by cute animal videos when going to check an email, for example. The satisfaction of opening a notification bubble gives us a little hit of dopamine, of feeling like we've 'completed' a task, instead of the one we actually intended to complete. Though we can chase this easy high all day long, it is the equivalent of binging on junk food for our minds.

This is because the highs are accompanied by lows. It is fraught with comparisons to others and an overload of unnecessary information, overwhelming our brains. We simply do not need to know what our friends ate for breakfast or how the weather is on the other side of the world. As a virtual rabbit hole in which we can go searching for our own unique insecurities to compare our lives to, it can be terrible for our self-esteem. It can help us to avoid our own feelings by providing an easy source of distraction - leaving us feeling numb.

Whilst there are certain benefits to social media such as connections with others, it is best for us to choose when we want to use it - rather than be drawn into using it when we should be doing something else. With so many different notifications and lives to keep track of on one device, it is naturally bound to fragment our attention into lots of little pieces.

I have always asked friends to change my passwords to my social media accounts when I have needed to focus during significant periods of my life, such as for the month before any exams, which was always very effective. Deleting some accounts completely has also been very helpful in terms of removing addictive distractions that were only making me feel negatively, such as Facebook.

There are various different ways of controlling how you use social media, rather than being controlled by it:

1. Assess how much you use social media. You can look at your 'screen time' if your phone has this feature – the amount of hours that you spend scrolling might shock you!

2. Make an overall assessment of your social media habit. Notice how you feel after going on it, who you follow,

what your purposes in using it are. How does the thought of not being able to use it for a day make you feel? If it is anxious and worried, that is a good signal that you need a break.

3. Clean up your accounts. Choose to only follow people who make you feel happy and are bring good quality content into your life. Don't feel bad about unfollowing – see 'N is for No' for more on people pleasing. If you don't want to unfollow your friends but their content makes you feel negative, you could mute them.

4. Decrease the amount of time you mindlessly spend on social media. There are a variety of options available to you:

- ❑ Dedicate yourself a certain time during the day in which you can go on social media, and stick to it!
- ❑ Delete the apps from your phone.
- ❑ Deactivate your accounts. This will usually hold your information until you reactivate again in the future, but double check!
- ❑ Delete your accounts all together, which should remove your information permanently.
- ❑ Ask a friend to change your passwords for you.
- ❑ Charge your phone in a different room to the one you sleep in. Try not to use it when you don't need it.
- ❑ See if any of your friends want to do a social media cleanse together. It can be helpful to be kept accountable!

Remove all distractions

Our focus is greatly improved by removing distractions. This means anything that draws your attention away from the task you want to focus on - such as other people, emails, or sounds such as the radio.

Your own mind might be the distraction. Try to simply notice every time that your mind wanders from what you are trying to do, and bring it back to the present moment – without beating yourself up for it! Meditating on your breath is also a good way to gain control of your thoughts and learn how to focus sustained attention on one thing, in addition to clearing your mind.

If your workplace is distracting, for example with people often coming to speak to you or emails popping up, consider asking your employer for reasonable adjustments for your ADHD. This doesn't necessarily have to involve talking about your ADHD, but it could be as simple as asking to move to a quieter part of the office so that you can work in peace, or asking for a work from home day once a week.

It is also helpful to put 'focus' slots in to your diary so that if you have a shared calendar, other people can see that you are not to be disturbed during that time. You can put an automatic reply 'out of office' message on your emails and dedicate a certain portion of the day to different focuses.

Understand yourself

We all tend to have different bouts of energy throughout the day. Some people may work best in the morning whilst others may be extremely productive at night. ADHD is commonly associated with sleep problems, as in 'S is for Sleep', where we may feel hyper-active and productive!

We also may also learn and focus best in a particular way, which may be important to understand about yourself if you have ADHD and struggle with 'conventional' methods of learning. For example, I can focus by writing things down, whereas a friend of mine learns by walking around and reading things out loud. You could learn by physically 'doing' things or making connections between certain concepts. I connected the case law names in my degree to fictional stories that I made up to relate to the facts which always helped me to remember them, which might sound like an extra layer of complication to anybody else!

Diet can also have an effect on our ability to focus, as can medication and exercise. To focus on something for a sustained period, we want to avoid short bursts of energy followed by depletion, which means avoiding sugar and caffeine as in 'M is for Medication'.

To understand how you focus best:

1. Think about when you have been able to focus successfully in the past. What enabled you to focus so well – how did you learn? Try to remember as much as you can and write it down in a list.

2. Consider activities that you do and do not enjoy doing. What is the reason that you find something 'boring' or 'fun'?

3. Think about how you can apply your own focus technique to boring activities, and anything that you might have to do to prepare for this.

Timing

As we will see in 'T is for Time Management', timing is ultimately key to managing our ADHD and planning out our lives accordingly. It is when we run out of time, or think we don't have enough, that we rush and make mistakes.

ADHD-ers also react to timelines, pressure and deadlines. They tend to not react so well so stress, so it is a good idea to always leave as much time as possible. If you can start something now instead of in six weeks, start it now. Become ultra-organised and set your own deadlines to motivate yourself. Break down a task into different parts and set yourself a deadline for each of these. With enough time and broken down, the overwhelming mountain of a task will become an easy, manageable part of your day.

It is also good to train your focus using timing. The Pomodoro technique has been proven to increase productivity, by setting a timer for 25 minutes in which to focus and taking a 5 minute break. Like high-intensity interval training, but for your mind. The concept can be adjusted to whatever task you are trying to get done, for example, setting at timer for 5 minutes to do the washing up. Self-motivation is simply *forcing* yourself to do something and engaging those executive functions.

Incentivise yourself

The best way to make yourself do something that you don't want to do, is to figure out how you *would* want to do it. How can you turn going to the dentist into a positive activity? Everybody is motivated differently, so the best way to figure out how to incentivise yourself is to think about what you enjoy, and what motivates you in life.

Essentially, you are tricking yourself as though you were a toddler who doesn't want to eat their broccoli. You can either hide the broccoli in different food or hold the dessert hostage. By eating the broccoli first, you can enjoy the things you want to enjoy properly. This is a concept known as delayed gratification.

Be kind to yourself

Perfection is a glass ceiling. If we held perfection up as a standard goal, nothing would ever get done. We can hold ourselves accountable to doing something perfectly or not at all, and equate finishing something with it being 'perfect'. A fear of being unable to meet impossible standards may make us more prone to becoming distracted and not having to actually finish what we start, because that can feel much more scary in exposing ourself to potential judgment and rejection.

Done is better than perfect.

Instead of 'perfect', aim for done. Once something is done, then you can perfect it – if you want to! Chapter 'K is for Kindness' explains how we can be kind to ourselves and gently support ourselves through doing something tricky. By speaking to yourself negatively when you procrastinate, you are perpetuating a cycle of anxiety and self-hatred that will keep you in the same place instead of actually getting anything done at all.

Trying something is the only way you will improve at it – nobody starts out perfect. We are all human, and nobody is born good at everything. Skills come from practice, and sustained effort, which can be done by anyone - whether they have ADHD or not.

Having ADHD does not mean that you are doomed to never be good enough to do anything. It doesn't mean that you should just give up before even trying – on the contrary, ADHD can be seen as a 'superpower', as in 'W is for Weaknesses'. It enables you to think differently to neurotypical people, with more energy than most, that you can translate into incredible achievements. Once you understand how to manage over-active thoughts, you can choose to dedicate the immense power of your brain to anything you want to focus on.

is for quitting

Did you know?

- People with ADHD have been reported to be more likely to quit a job because of dislike than those without (Kuriyan et al, 2013).

- A study found that 32.2% of students with the combined type of ADHD drop out of high school, compared to 15% of teenagers with no psychiatric disorder (Breslau et al, 2011).

- Research has suggested that university students in the UK do not receive enough support, finding it is usually limited to that which would be provided for students with dyslexia, which can result in them dropping out (Attention UK).

This chapter is about quitting, but also committing. As ADHD-ers tend to be impulsive and have short attention spans, they may commonly find themselves in situations where they start new projects regularly and energetically, but can't keep up this level of determination and quit. The quitting tends to feed into the cycle of low self-esteem and feeling 'not good enough', resulting in impacted relationships with others and general exhaustion.

I used to live in fear of starting anything because I didn't trust myself to finish anything. It was very frustrating being unable to control which new ideas I would put into life on any given day, before getting bored of them a week later. Living in this way perpetuates the short attention span and limiting beliefs that can accompany ADHD of not being able to finish anything that we start.

How to commit to something

The secret of committing to something is taking the time to think about it carefully before starting it. We can see this in 'N is for No', where our brains essentially make decisions so quickly that we can end up saying yes to things we don't actually want to do.

Ultimately, this simply involves us thinking something through from different angles than the 'I want to do this right now' one - which can be very persuasive! When we are feeling inspired, we might think that we can do anything, until we learn how much commitment it actually involves.

When you are considering a new project, try to think about it in terms of whether you actually, realistically *want* to do it, with full knowledge of what it will involve. Consider whether you have the time, finances and resources available to you to do this project on a long-term basis. Take caution in telling other people and try to think things through double as long if other people are involved in this project. It is often setting the expectations to others that is our downfall, as our creative ideas can sound brilliant as a concept and much harder once someone has agreed to work with us on the practical reality of it.

After this, if you decide that you actually want to do something, then set yourself a time limit. This is a specific (short!) amount of time to stay no matter what - within reason. Try to keep your time limit realistic and achievable, such as one month in a new job. This should be weighed up against the potential implications of quitting - if you want to try a new hobby, then you should feel free to quit this whenever you want to, without feeling badly about it. Our tendency to do things for as long as we want to can actually mean that we live very authentic lives, because we are living in line with our morals and beliefs, but if we make commitments that involve other people or are objectively good for us to keep, we should try our best to honour them.

Another key aspect of commitment is making it as easy as possible for yourself. Try to identify in advance what your 'triggers' are – why have you quit things in the past? Do you struggle with organisation or certain types of people? Plan out in advance a plan of how you can deal with these triggers and make it as easy as possible, such as finding a therapist for a certain period of time to help you transition. As we will see in 'T is for Time Management', the key to this is taking things as slowly as possible, and giving ourselves more time than we think we need.

Finally, do not place any additional expectations on yourself. ADHD-ers can start things very enthusiastically, before realising how much effort is involved. This might mean not telling as many people about your new idea as you would want to, not sharing it on social media until it is ready to be shared, not over-promising... just taking things as slowly as possible.

Once you are in the project, treat it as a learning experience. You might not stay in it forever, but you can learn from every single experience. In fact you are unlikely to stay in any project for ever – we are living longer and many people have two or three careers in their lives! Remember to be kind to yourself as in 'K is for Kindness' and that you are not trapped in anything.

When to quit

If something is making you more unhappy than happy, then you should certainly quit. However, ADHD-ers can tend to quit things as easily as they start them, which can often be impulsive, emotional decisions that they can regret. The key to this again, is patience as in 'T is for Time Management' - thinking over all of our decisions, whether to start or quit something.

You do not have to quit something the moment that you are unhappy or feel overwhelmed with emotion, as in 'R is for Rejection'. You can wait it through and grow your resilience muscle, testing yourself and growing as a person, proving to yourself that you can *choose* to quit something rather than have it all happen before you even know what is going on.

Having ADHD can be extremely emotionally overwhelming. The best thing to do when you feel overwhelmed is to remove yourself from the situation, be kind to yourself and rest. Taking a break from a stressful situation will give you the literal and metaphorical space to think things though and process your feelings.

It is good to examine your feelings about quitting in the same way as you would when starting something. Look at it from all of the different angles and consider the impact it will have on you long-term - on your finances, overall happiness levels and life. Try to think about the alternatives – what would the benefits of not quitting be?

When you are feeling overwhelmed it can be hard to imagine feeling any differently about a situation, but a good rule of thumb is to give it at least a week.

However, if a situation is causing you significant stress or putting you in danger, then leave. You should be able to weigh up whether something is seriously harming you or just stressing you out. Difficult experiences can lead to growth, but putting yourself through significant harm or in danger is never a good idea – always leave as soon as possible in this situation. You do not owe anybody anything in terms of being exploited. Manipulators can recognise people pleasing tendencies, as in 'N is for No', and expertly make you feel guilty for 'leading them on', in full knowledge of what they are doing.

Similarly, weigh up situations on the pros and cons. Staying in a job for a year can have different benefits to say, staying in a negative hobby. For example, I joined a professional cheerleading club and hated it, but felt too guilty to quit, having convinced a friend to join with me and committed to a competition. Instead of leaving, I moaned to my friend and half-heartedly attended sessions out of sufferance for months, until quitting just before the competition out of anxiety that I would ruin it for the whole team! It's good to see your time as money – if one reason for continuing something you don't enjoy is because you've invested into it, you are simply wasting more of your time and money.

By quitting, you are ultimately taking responsibility for your own happiness. You can't look to other people to give you permission to leave or create excuses so that you can go – you just need to accept that you don't want to do it anymore and go. It's like ripping off a plaster in that it can be awkward and painful at the time, but is over before you know it. Everyone tends to be much more grateful when you just quit something that you really do not want to do, because you aren't wasting anybody's time.

How to quit

We may feel a lot of shame over quitting things. ADHD-ers tend to overthink a lot and can find themselves catastrophising the 'quitting' process far beyond what it needs to be, replaying previous experiences of failures over in our heads.

Ultimately, people just don't care that much. Even if you leave a relationship, the other person will find happiness again, and it's better for them to be with someone who actually feels the same way. You can be replaced in the workplace, as scary as that feels. It is unlikely to make a material difference to anyone else's life if you start up your own business and close it two days later. Most people are far too busy worrying about themselves to concern themselves too much with your quitting.

This being said, it is good to not 'burn bridges', if you can help it. The emotional mood swings associated with ADHD can trigger acting before thinking, particularly impulsive actions that you can later regret. For example, walking out of a job because you have had a fight with your colleague only reflects badly on you, and may make it difficult to get a reference in the future. Taking a calmer approach, and leaving a job when you feel ready to, in a respectful, upfront and calm manner, is more likely to result in your employer supporting you how they can.

This ultimately requires you to not take things personally, as we will see in 'R is for Rejection'. It requires you to dust off those executive functioning tools in your brain and implement patience, removing yourself emotionally from the situation.

How to quit something

- When you feel ready to quit something, give yourself a week. Allow yourself an additional week of knowing you are planning to quit, but don't tell anyone during that time. If you still want to quit at the end of the week, go ahead and proceed. Try to imagine how you will feel about the situation in 6 months, and 1 years' time.

- Try to only tell a select few people that you trust, ideally outside of the situation.

- Consider alternatives. For example, if you want to quit a job because of difficulty with your ADHD-symptoms, consider disclosing your ADHD to your employer, as in 'J is for Jobs', so that they can make reasonable accommodations for you.

- Behave appropriately and respectfully. This will usually mean being as communicative and upfront as possible, for example by ending a relationship face to face.

- Be honest. Do not overly apologise or appropriate more blame to yourself than you have to, but stand your ground and explain your reasoning clearly.

- Make this as easy as possible for yourself. Things that could help include speaking to someone you trust about the situation first, who can help you to quit, or writing down the reasons you want to quit so you have it to hand in case you feel overwhelmed.

- ❑ Offer to complete any existing obligations to the people involved. This could be working out your notice period, or finding someone to replace you in a rental agreement, for example.

- ❑ Maintain your boundaries – if you want to quit and someone is not accepting this, remember that you have every right to quit and no one deserves to make you feel otherwise. Do not let people guilt you into doing something you don't want to do – especially if this is harming you!

is for rejection

Did you know?

- Dr William Dodson coined the phrased 'Rejection Sensitive Dysphoria' (RSD), finding that it appears to be the one emotional condition that is found only with ADHD. This can result in a person being triggered to feel extreme pain by real or perceived rejection, is said to be genetic and neurological, and lasts for very short periods of time (Dodson, Emotional Regulation and Rejection Sensitivity, 2016).

- If this emotional response is internalised, it can appear as instantaneous but triggered major depression. If it is externalised, it can manifest as rage at another person or situation - 50% of people who are court mandated for anger management treatment have previously unrecognised ADHD. RSD can result in a misdiagnosis of ADHD, as it is still a relatively new concept (Dodson, Emotional Regulation and Rejection Sensitivity, 2016).

- It has been reported that nearly 1 in 3 people with ADHD say that RSD is the hardest part of living with ADHD (Bhandari, What Is Rejection Sensitive Dysphoria?, 2020).

Rejection Sensitive Dysphoria (RSD) is commonly linked to ADHD. This refers to the extreme emotional sensitivity and pain that a person with RSD may feel when triggered by the perception of being rejected. Whilst nobody likes being rejected, this is the one emotional symptom that has only been associated with ADHD as opposed to other conditions. Dr William Dodson says it is genetic and neurological, but it may also come from people with ADHD being typecast as 'lazy' or a failure in the past. RSD can be expressed outwards in intense bursts of rage and impulsive decision making, or internalised by a person, causing them to feel so overwhelmed that they may even feel suicidal.

It feels like an overwhelming rush of emotion that overloads your system so much that you just want to turn it off in any way that you can. When you calm down, the feelings go away very quickly, but it can be very scary and upsetting to experience, especially if you don't know about RSD and why it is happening. It is the worst feeling in the world when you feel the wave of emotions quite literally take over your body – as though you lack control over your mind, almost like an emotional panic attack.

RSD can result in ADHD-ers becoming people pleasers, suffering from a lot of anxiety. They may constantly try to anticipate what everyone around them wants, searching for guidance in others instead of living their own life. They may become obsessed with keeping the overwhelming feelings at bay by taking responsibility for the feelings of others, in the hope of not being rejected.

It can also result in depression. People with RSD may simply stop trying to do anything, failing to see the point in applying for a job or seeing people they care about, because of the exposure to potential rejection. They may be chronic underachievers as a result and be consistently unhappy.

Contrastingly, RSD could manifest as unrealistically high standards of perfection, as in 'H is for High-functioning'. These people can suffer from exactly the same utter lack of self-esteem, but mask it with punishing themselves into overworking or holding a 'glass ceiling' of achievements over their head, meaning that they will never be happy. They might think that when they achieve 'X' they will 'deserve' happiness, but X might be virtually impossible to achieve.

Another aspect of RSD is self-sabotaging, as in 'Q is for Quitting'. It can unfortunately lead to many impulsive, emotionally charged decisions that can make you feel guilty and embarrassed afterwards, blaming yourself in a never-ending cycle, that ironically feels very lonely.

Our personal relations with others can suffer dramatically as a result of RSD. People pleasing tends to often backfire, or result in toxic relationships being prioritised above those who genuinely care for us. Nobody will ever be able to convince you that they will always like you, and so we may be prone to having an 'insecure attachment style' in all of our relationships and feel constantly anxious in relation to others, as in 'L is for Love'.

As in 'X is for X-rated', romantic relationships can also be impacted significantly as a result of being hyper-sensitive to rejection. Our partners can be bewildered at our overreactions to small things, such as them texting back after a few hours or lateness. They may be confused as to why their assurances of how much they like us are never enough and they have to keep trying to prove it. They may not understand why we think we are so difficult to love and in the end, believe what we say – a self-fulfilling prophecy. Our anticipation of rejection can sadly lead us to self-sabotage good relationships with people that do genuinely care about us.

Relationships that are overshadowed by feelings of anticipated rejection tend to be volatile and result in someone with RSD feeling that love is 'conditional'. The ironic cruelty of RSD is that the sufferer can often reject others in the hope of protecting themselves. Feelings of potential rejection can lead to dramatic, impulsive decisions such as quitting a job or cutting somebody out of our lives without thinking – sometimes in the ill-conceived hope of the other person showing that they care.

Having ADHD and RSD is incredibly lonely. It means you are struggling with all of the symptoms of ADHD in this vacuum of loneliness, where you might believe that nobody truly cares about you. The symptoms bounce off each other – not being able to complete things due to insecurity of previous failures and an inability to ask for help, exacerbated by perceived loneliness and rejecting everyone as a result.

RSD can also manifest physically. Our bodies might react to the perceived threat of rejection by becoming unwell, overly tired or hyperactive. Some people may shut off completely and find it very difficult to formulate words to express how they are feeling, which can be very frustrating for the people around them.

It is very difficult to treat RSD as it hits so quickly, and the emotions can overwhelm a person so suddenly that they can find themselves experiencing it at the same rate as everybody else. ADHD medication has helped me with RSD to the extent that it make me feel more confident in tackling life and so intercepted part of the cycle mentioned above. The psychological feeling of taking medication helped me to feel that I was *capable* of having a stable life, so I did not perceive potential rejection as a life ruining concept in and of itself. I had found stability that could theoretically remain whether somebody liked me or not. Ultimately, the key to dealing with rejection is to build up your self-esteem so that it is not reliant on the acceptance of other people, just yourself.

Reframing our thoughts

The perception of rejection can be so overwhelming that we act without thinking, when often there may not have even been any rejection in the first place! I would equate this to 'gas-lighting' yourself, imagining scenarios that aren't really happening and driving yourself to act erratically.

This boils down to a lack of trust in others to like us for who we are. When we start liking ourselves, then we start to understand that we are pretty great as we are and do not need to 'do' anything for others to like us.

In addition to learning the art of patience and slowing down our thoughts, we can also learn to interject rational thoughts amongst the hurricane of emotions. We have to train ourselves to literally trust other people to like us and for that to be our automatic thought as opposed to searching for all of the reasons that people wouldn't like us. This can be done by staying aware of our tendencies to perceive rejection and actively combatting any worries, reminding ourselves that we are liked and accepted.

Managing RSD

1. Think about a time you have experienced RSD previously and have been overwhelmed by your own emotions. What triggered the RSD and what helped you?

2. Make a list of triggers, of things that you perceive as rejection from others. This could include anything

from feeling excluded in social settings, to somebody not replying to your messages for several hours.

3. Create a list of things that make you feel calm, happy and secure. These could include activities such as cooking, bubble baths, reading a book, or having a massage, for example. When you are feeling overwhelmed, try to do one of these activities as soon as possible.

4. Hack your life to reduce the number of triggers and increase the number and accessibility of things that make you feel secure. For example, if unresponsive communication styles trigger you, avoid dating people who have problems with communication. Or if you feel secure by doing yoga, sign up to a gym or appoint a space that you can go and do yoga in when you are feeling triggered.

5. When you are feeling triggered, train your brain to look for the secure things first. If this happens a lot, maybe keep a list on you at all times. Do something that makes you feel secure, such as calling a friend, before doing anything else. Train this to be your automatic response.

6. If you are feeling overwhelmed by RSD, remind yourself that you are experiencing RSD as a result of your ADHD, which will soon pass. Try to leave any situations as soon as possible to calm down and be as kind as possible to yourself, doing one of your 'secure' activities. It's a good idea to try and distract yourself until the feelings have passed, such as by watching a film or reading a book.

7. Use a mood tracker app or journal to regularly record your feelings. Find all of the opposite reasons to what your thoughts are telling you in relation to potential rejection from others. For example, if you think that someone doesn't like you, find all of the proof that they do like you.

Having RSD does not mean that there is anything wrong with you. It means that you feel things on a deeper level than most and as a result, tend to be more compassionate. Understanding the stress and emotions that your body can experience in one go means that you tend to be good at understanding the stress of other people, as it arises in small manageable chunks! Remember to be kind to yourself, no matter what. You are deserving of love and the people around you will love you unconditionally, even if it doesn't always feel that way.

is for sleep

Did you know?

- ADHD has been called a '24 hour disorder' by researchers (Weiss et McBride, 2018). Almost 3 out of 4 children and adolescents, and up to 4 out of 5 adults with ADHD have a sleep disorder. ADHD can affect our 'circadian rhythm' (sleep-wake cycle), potentially making it harder to fall asleep or causing disruptions throughout the night, making it difficult to wake up and function well throughout the day without falling asleep.

- A study has shown that there is a lot of crossover between symptoms of ADHD and narcolepsy, such as excessive daytime sleepiness and inattention (Oosterloo, 2018). The high symptom overlap suggests that both conditions could be misdiagnosed.

- Researchers have related ADHD to interest-based performance, finding that ADHD-ers can be at risk of falling asleep when they are bored, if their nervous system disengages. This can be very dangerous if it occurs at inappropriate times, such as when driving. (Dodson, 2020)

ADHD-ers commonly encounter difficulty sleeping. 75% of adults with ADHD have been reported to experience insomnia (Dodson, 2020). Our minds might race with thoughts late at night or we might have more energy in the evening, making it difficult to get to sleep. If you take stimulant medication, this also can keep you awake throughout the night, making you feel wired. As a result, you are likely to be tired throughout the day. The general stress associated with ADHD would have an effect on anybody's sleeping patterns!

ADHD symptoms tend to become a lot worse without enough sleep, and there's a lot of crossover between ADHD and sleep conditions such as narcolepsy, causing potential misdiagnosis. Executive functioning and self-motivation become much harder without the basic necessity of good sleep and energy. Sleep problems can manifest differently in different people, and seem to become worse in ADHD-ers with age. Researchers have found that before puberty, 10-15% of children with ADHD have trouble falling asleep, by age 12.5 this is 50%, and by age 30, it's more than 70% (Dodson, 2020).

Difficulty falling asleep

As ADHD-ers are known to have racing minds and find it hard to sit still, the thought of actually shutting down our bodies for sleep can seem impossible. This is even more so if we have spent our days in a buzz of distraction or hyper-focus, ignoring any stresses that we might be feeling. The minute we lie down in the dark the thoughts can all pour into our heads, and we can be hit with a sense of energy compelling us to 'do' something to avoid all of these feelings. As in 'Y is for Your Body', we might also be oblivious to physical discomfort throughout the day which could manifest as pain when we go to sleep, such as poor posture whilst sitting.

The thing that many people 'do' is go on their phones - it is usually accessible, nearby and perfectly absorbs our attention. Evidence has proven the link between screen time at night to greater problems related to sleep for adolescents with ADHD (Becker & Lienesch, 2018).

Problems with falling asleep can become worse with age, I expect because we have more to worry about! It can be very frustrating to experience as your mind literally races with thoughts, whilst you try to make yourself fall asleep. Common ADHD medication is stimulant based, which can also keep us awake, especially if we combine it with other stimulants such as caffeine.

Having an evening routine, as in 'G is for Grounding' is very helpful in terms of falling asleep. This might involve turning screens off at least one hour before bed, time to de-compress after the day, and avoiding any stimulants after a certain time, for example.

Restless sleep

ADHD brains might stay activated throughout the night, waking us up with incessant thinking about the things we need to do. We then face the problem of falling back asleep all over again! We may also be quite uncomfortable to sleep next to if our physical hyperactivity remains throughout the night, for example by tossing and turning. As in 'Y is for Your Body', physical symptoms can accompany ADHD such as 'restless leg syndrome' or a need to keep moving.

This impacts on the quality of our sleep and can cause us to feel tired the next day. One particularly annoying thing I experience is waking up in the night but being half asleep, so unable to move physically but inundated with thoughts and worries. This has been referred to as sleep paralysis. It's hard to tell how long it lasts, so even if it is only for a few minutes, I can wake up feeling as though I have had been awake all night.

This is especially worse for me if I am particularly hyper-focused on something or feeling stressed - I will often wake up in the night 'working' in my brain, or wake myself up with thoughts about work!

It can be helpful to try different options out in terms of what can help with this. Meditation, as in 'Z is for Zen', can calm down our nervous system and routines that avoid stimulating our brains too much, such as reading a pleasant, non-addictive fiction book. I also find weighted and electronic blankets to help, and 'falling back to sleep' meditations - but these do require going on my phone, so a lot of willpower not to go on anything else!

Difficulty waking up and staying awake

It can also be hard for ADHD-ers to wake up when they are supposed to. This may be because of the difficulty in actually managing to sleep, making us feel exhausted and reluctant to go through the entire process again. Our internal clock may not recognise the hours that we are 'supposed' to sleep and be awake, seeing it as another box of society to fit into. This cycle leads to ADHD-ers being exhausted throughout the day and with less energy than other people, when we tend to need a lot more to help regulate our brains in the same way.

We may also have trouble with staying awake. I used to regularly fall asleep in school classes despite not having particular problems with sleep at night. It has been suggested that if a person with ADHD doesn't have interest in an activity, their nervous system can disengage to a point that is so abrupt to induce sudden extreme drowsiness and falling asleep. We can literally fall asleep from being bored, which can be life-threatening if we happen to be driving (Paul Wender MD, 2020).

Improving the quality of our sleep can help with staying awake throughout the day. If you are affected by falling asleep at inappropriate times, then it is advisable not to drive or do anything that can be dangerous to do if you aren't fully awake, such as operate heavy machinery. In the UK, ADHD-ers have a duty to disclose their ADHD if it affects their ability to drive safely (Driver and Vehicle Licensing Agency, 2020).

Improving our sleep

The issue is ultimately trouble with relaxing and switching off. As we will see in 'Z is for Zen', there are a variety of ways that you can do this, but a good way to approach sleep generally is to apply the concepts we have used in this book to it. We need to make our goals realistic and achievable, and to be kind to ourselves. We need to reduce the overall stress and think about how we can 'hack' ourselves to actually truly want to sleep, how to reduce the pressure and expectations we put on ourselves. We need to stop thinking that there is something wrong with us or getting angry when we can't sleep, because this just heightens the emotional cycle of frustration.

To do this, we can look at our own specific sleep patterns and make a strategy:

1. Make an assessment of your sleeping patterns. Write down:
    - ❑ How many hours of sleep you typically get a night
    - ❑ Any problems you have associated with getting to sleep, staying asleep or waking up

- ❑ What is behind these problems – for example, if your mind is racing, what are you generally thinking about?

- ❑ How tired you feel throughout the day

- ❑ How stressed you are in general and why

- ❑ What you equate to a good night's sleep. Think about the details – do you prefer to be hot or cold? Do you prefer to sleep alone or to have company? To go to sleep early or late? To have lights or sounds on or off?

2. Make a list of your barriers to a good night's sleep and try to think of solutions to these. For example:

    - ❑ Dislike being cold: use a hot water bottle or electric blanket

    - ❑ Dislike being too hot: use a fan or invest in a lighter duvet

    - ❑ Distracted by lights / sounds: use 'white noise' apps, earplugs, or use an eye-mask

    - ❑ Can't switch off thoughts: meditate before sleep, or listen to an audio-book Avoid stimulants such as caffeine before bed.

    - ❑ Stressed out: find a therapist, as in 'M is for Medication'.

    - ❑ Going on your phone in the night: charge it in a different room

- ❏ Trouble waking up: invest in an alarm clock that suits your particular needs, for example one that runs around the room!

- ❏ If there are any that you can't find a solution to, google them! There is a solution for every problem. Don't let your brain find excuses such as 'I can't afford X'. Sleep should be your number one priority – you won't be able to work as well without it!

3. Create a 'sleep routine' as in 'G is for Grounding', using your lists as the basis. Make yourself a routine including:

    - ❏ What time you turn off your electronics each evening – screens, phones and so on.

    - ❏ Where you will charge your electronics each night whilst you sleep (as far away as possible!)

    - ❏ The things that you will do before bed, such as meditating, reading, writing or exercise.

    - ❏ What time you will go to bed – try to make this the same each evening.

    - ❏ What time you will wake up – as above, try to make this the same, even on the weekends.

    - ❏ Having a routine that you don't have to think about too much will allow you to do these things on autopilot and signal to your body that it is time to shut down. You are a human being designed for sleep – you are capable of sleeping peacefully for 8 hours each evening, you just need to train yourself how to do it right according to you. Make sure that the routine is easy and achievable and be kind to yourself if you don't follow it one evening – just start again!

Tips

- ❏ Charge your phone in a different room. Phones are the number one distraction for us and are so easy to go on in the night, scrolling for hours. It is also really unhealthy to scroll for hours first thing in the morning, stopping you from getting out of bed! Make it as difficult as possible for yourself to access your phone when you are supposed to be sleeping and don't let your mind think of excuses – you can buy an alarm clock or invest in a CD recording of meditations, for example.

- ❏ If you are truly unable to charge it in a different room, make sure it is on aeroplane mode at night! Nobody needs to contact you when you are asleep.

- ❏ Avoid going on your phone for at least one hour before bed each night. Our phones are perfect for engineering racing thoughts, overloading our brains with information that we simply do not need.

- ❏ Set a 'bed time' and stick to it for a week. Don't pressure yourself to sleep when you are in bed, just lie there and try to count or play games with yourself. Things that help me to get to sleep are listing every single thing that happened in my day factually (without stressing about it!), thinking of words in different categories from A to Z and counting the number of breaths I can do into my stomach.

- ❑ Try to do something before bed each evening that switches your mind off. This could be reading a book (make sure it's not too addictive!), writing, meditating or yoga, for example. Avoid television or watching something on a screen, because the light will affect your brain and may make it think it is still day time.

- ❑ Invest in different things to promote a good night's sleep. I use an electric blanket, hot water bottle, weighted blanket, furry duvet covers and a sunlight emulating alarm clock. Some people may benefit from essential oil humidifiers, white noise creators, eye masks, ear plugs or fans – I am sure there are many more!

- ❑ Do not be afraid to try sleep medication and vitamins. Speak to your Doctor about what may be best for you.

- ❑ Make sure that you are eating a healthy, balanced diet as in 'M is for Medication'. Reduce the amount of caffeine or sugar that you consume throughout the day to encourage your brain to slow down towards the evening.

- ❑ Remember that you are not alone and there is nothing wrong with you for not being able to sleep. It is perfectly natural that we would want to stay awake if our minds are not ready to turn off, but we will try to help ourselves switch them off because we know it is going to be better for us in the long run. Be kind to yourself.

- ❑ At the same time, be strict with your thoughts. If you find yourself lying awake, ruminating on something that you don't need to be thinking about, firmly tell yourself that 'now is not the time to be thinking about this' and choose to focus on something else.

❑ Think about speaking to your workplace, as in 'J is for Jobs', about flexible working hours if you find that you have more energy at a certain time of day.

❑ See 'P is for Procrastination' on tips for how to get up in the morning – the secret is just forcing yourself to do it, nothing more! Count to 5 and make yourself uncomfortable for a second, hop out of bed and face the day. I have a 'getting out of bed' playlist that helps motivate me!

is for time management

Did you know?

- Research has proven that people with ADHD have difficulties in being able to assess time, and feel as though time is passing them by without being able to complete tasks accurately and well. These skills are said to be critical for effective time management (Ptacek et al, 2019).

- People with ADHD tend to be very heavily influenced by their external surroundings, and can struggle with future-planning. We can have a sense of time that is 'now' or 'not now' (Ptacek et al, 2019).

- Medical treatment of ADHD has been found to normalise time perception.

ADHD is very strongly linked with problems relating to time management. This is because we tend to only have two senses of time: now, and not now. This chapter is focused on building in a pause between an 'event' and what we plan to do about it, because for people with ADHD, there is no pause. The make-up of our brains mean that we respond automatically, seemingly without thinking - or at least very quickly.

Dr Barkley explains the impact that ADHD has on our executive functions very well (Barkley, 2017):

1. Hindsight: when faced with a decision, ADHD-ers cannot visualise the relevant past in their mind's eye. We don't have the theatre in our minds that allow us to replay our previous experiences out as others do.

2. Foresight: as a result of being unable to look back, we are unable to anticipate the future. We can't look back

and plan for the future, because we have no context within which to come up with these thoughts.

3. Mental voice: ADHD also impacts the brain in a way so that we cannot hear our 'minds voice', the self-parenting voice that tells us to make 'sensible' choices instead of what we automatically want to do. This is why we struggle following instructions or rules - the voices that are supposed to regulate us don't show up in our brains.

4. Mind's heart: our emotions are our motivations, and if we cannot manage our emotions, then we cannot manage our motivations either. Our emotions are the fuel tank for all future directed behaviour, and so this is why ADHD-ers cannot motivate themselves like those without it can. Our motivation of how long and hard we can work will always be dependent on our environment and its immediate consequences. If there are no consequences for us, then we cannot focus.

Dr Barkley compares homework, the completion of a maths problem on paper, with playing video games. The latter provides a constant source of external simulation and consequences, whereas doing our homework, we would have to wait until the next day to feel any external consequences. Maybe this is why I often did mine on the way to school!

5. Mind's playground: our ability to plan and problem solve. Due to the above impairments, ADHD-ers cannot think of multiple possible future options or solutions at the same time, which originates in problem solving.

Dr Barkley says we should try to minimise the time between events happening, the responses that we prepare, and the outcomes of what we are doing.

The concept of waiting between having a thought and acting on is what underpins many ADHD symptoms, such as impulsivity. It is literally not being able to think things through properly. We are directed by reason, consequences, and immediate external stimulus.

Figuring out how to use time helps us to think at the same level as other people and manage our energy in a sustainable, focused way. When we take the time to think things through, we are better able to predict our own capacity to do something, instead of over-committing. We may find that we need to delegate work or ask for help from others, which helps us to manage our own time better. When we are able to stop taking on things that are not our responsibility, we can pay proper attention and focus to the things that are.

Having ADHD means that we have to train our brains in *patience*. It can feel hard not to want to do everything at once, or not at all, but this ultimately requires us to trust ourselves in being able to manage our time and energy appropriately so that we don't burn ourselves out. We don't always need to reply to every email or request immediately. We can wait, think about it and return to it when we are ready.

This time gap specifically allocated for 'thinking' is where we should try to exercise our skills in considering something from various angles. To do this, I would recommend trying to delay any decisions until you are able to make the following considerations:

- Our past: try to remember any similar situations that you have encountered previously, how you felt about them, and any lessons learned. For example, saying yes to something you didn't really want to do, letting somebody down and feeling guilty as a result.

- Our future: what will this situation look like in one week, month or years' time? Do we have any pre-existing commitments that could cause a conflict with this decision? Would we still want to be doing this in a year, for example?

- What the decision will involve in reality: the boring bits. For example, if we are considering a new job, have we thought through all of the potentially negative aspects, as well as the positive? Have we thought about what our daily life will look like, our commute, colleagues, workload? Do we have any notice periods to work through?

- Other people: how might our decision impact others? For example, if we are considering moving to a new country, how would this impact our partner, or family?

- Potentially negative consequences: weighing up the good against the bad. For example, if we are lending money to someone, what will we do if they are unable to return it? Is there any way we can take practical steps to plan for such a situation? How long-lasting would the positive consequences be?

- Opportunity cost: what will this decision cost us? What could we use the time, energy or money for if we were not doing this? For example, if we were planning to spend £20 on takeout from a restaurant, what else could we use that £20 for?

- How long we have to make the decision: do we have to do it **right now**? (Hint: usually the answer will be no!). If you can take your time in deciding, take it. Things often look differently the next day.

- Whether we actually want to do it: this may involve checking in with ourselves and spotting any tension in our bodies. Does the thought of saying yes make you clench your jaw, for example? How do you **feel** about it?

How to manage your time

- Make a time management plan by using a calendar. The plan accounts for your time overall, how much time is spent at work and at home. By separating out your time into manageable, scheduled chunks in advance, you can set yourself key focuses for these areas, such as 'work on X' or 'relax'. It is good to have one of these to hand on your phone, computer or printed out on your wall.

- Dedicate some time each morning to planning your day and deciding what to prioritise, setting a 'to-do' list. Try to limit it to three manageable tasks per day, with the ones you don't want to do first. As ADHD-ers are externally motivated, it may be helpful to write this on a whiteboard and set yourself reminders such as scheduled alerts or post-it notes.

- Separate any general tasks into 'important but not urgent', 'important and urgent', 'urgent but not important', and 'not urgent and not important' lists. Prioritise those which are urgent and important and resolve to tackle the rest tomorrow. Write any distracting thoughts that pop up which are not urgent or important down on your list – it really helps to have them down on paper and out of your head!

- Spend a few days recording how long it takes you to complete different tasks, to gain a realistic understanding of time, and how long certain tasks take you to complete.

- Always remember to give yourself more time than you think you will need and to allocate time for breaks.

- Dedicate a certain amount of time each day to checking your emails, setting an automatic reply for other times. It is also very helpful to block in 'desk time' to your work calendar, so that you will not be disturbed or distracted.

- When planning time in relation to a specific project or deadline, set yourself a series of deadlines that will help you stay motivated. For example, these could be to finish a first draft on a certain date. It can be very helpful to have an 'accountability buddy' to do this with!

- When focusing on a project, concentrate on how to break this down into different sections and then break the sections down into individual tasks. Remember to appropriate each task to the relevant person – it is unlikely that you will have sole responsibility for a certain project without anyone else. Work with these people accordingly, setting realistic check in points for both of you – such as weekly phone calls – and don't be afraid to ask for help if you aren't sure.

is for unite

Did you know?

- The first All Party Parliamentary Group for ADHD launched in the Houses of Parliament in January 2018. At the time of writing, meetings are ongoing, with the aim of raising awareness about ADHD, bringing positive changes to the lives of people living with ADHD and to connect Parliament with organisations and charities involved in ADHD.

- There have been very successful campaigns such as the Umbrella Project, raising awareness about neurodiversity, as 1 in 5 people are neurodivergent (ADHD Foundation).

- There are ADHD focused communities and support groups available globally[9], where you can connect with other people who are having similar experiences to you. You are not alone.

Having ADHD can be extremely lonely and isolating. Strong interpersonal relationships can be very difficult to establish and maintain, due to the symptoms of ADHD such as emotional dysregulation and hyper-sensitivity to potential rejection.

These symptoms can be very lonely to experience, and it might be a revelation to even read a book such as this to see that you are not alone in how you are feeling. I was taken to a mental health meeting[10] in Australia by a friend and felt so relieved to see that other, seemingly 'normal' people were

---

[9] I recommend ADHD Unlocked: https://members.adhdunlocked.co.uk/~access/a1c91f/
[10] https://www.onewaveisallittakes.com/

having similar experiences to me. This can be particularly important if talking about mental health isn't something you are used to, or if the people in your life have some stigma towards it or ADHD in particular.

The reality is that millions of people throughout the world have ADHD and feel exactly the same way as you do. Around 1.5 million adults in the UK are estimated to have ADHD (ADHD Action, 2018), but only 120,000 are formally diagnosed. It can take up to seven years to be diagnosed in some parts of the UK, and this situation is similar worldwide. Around 6.4 million adults in America are said to have ADHD but do not enjoy access to free or subsidized healthcare as we do in the UK (Holland & Riley, 2014).

Long waiting times and financial constraints may mean that you are unable to be diagnosed with ADHD when you need to be, or access a therapist to talk to. This can feel like your life is on hold, especially if you feel that it is likely that you may have ADHD and want to take medication for it. I hope that this book has shown there are different ways of managing ADHD without the requirement for an official medical diagnosis.

Having a community that you can talk to about ADHD and your experiences without fearing that they will judge you is truly life changing. There are a variety of different ways that you could do this.

Unite: with friends

As seen in 'L is for Love', relationships with friends and family can become impacted by having ADHD. A great way of managing these is to identify one or two people closest to you, who you trust unconditionally, to be completely open with about the things that you are experiencing. Having someone that you know loves you and will be there for you unconditionally is a huge asset in fighting the feelings of low self-esteem and impulses to self-sabotage.

It can be difficult to open up to people, especially if you are seemingly a person who has everything under control as in 'H is for High-functioning', or struggle with finding the words to express your emotions. It might also feel a bit out of the blue and difficult to time correctly, but there will never be a good time. The best time is right now – you deserve to have connection with others right now.

Think about the best way to do this for you. Personally, I would recommend writing a letter to someone you trust, explaining how you feel and telling them how much you appreciate them being there for you. It is often easier to write out our feelings and be in control of what we want to say. You can send this to the person by post or meet up with them to give them the letter and have a conversation. Watch it change your life – the people around you are more perceptive than you think and are likely to be extremely grateful to you for opening up to them.

You may also find that your feelings are more common than you thought – as a human being, your experiences are literally the same as other people experience. We all have the same spectrum of emotions and anything you feel, it has been felt before. Being vulnerable around the people close to you allows them to be vulnerable in return and is the key to true connection.

It may also be that the people around you have similar experiences in relation to ADHD specifically. I have found that I tend to attract people with ADHD – probably because we understand each other's impulsivity, incessant talking and occasional interrupting!

As it is hereditary, it is likely that other people in your family have ADHD if you do. Think about who you want to discuss ADHD with carefully and try to pick someone who is calm and will prioritise you over any personal opinions they may have, such as feelings of defensiveness. I have found that discussing ADHD with people who are resistant to seeing it in themselves can sometimes be tricky, so pick wisely. Remember that having ADHD doesn't change who you are as a person, or define you.

Unite: with other people who have ADHD

There are communities of ADHD-ers all over the world. The brilliant thing about the internet is that it is literally easier than ever to find and communicate with people who share similar interests to you.

It can be very rewarding to speak to people who suffer with ADHD online, although it is important to make sure that you are safe and follow usual internet safety procedures, such as not giving away personal information or meeting people from the internet who you do not trust 100% - especially alone! Avoid meeting anyone from the internet in a private location and try to always take somebody else with you if you do plan to meet up.

As someone who is open about having ADHD on the internet, this could make you a target to people who want to manipulate you, who can use ADHD as a commonality between you. They may understand how to play on your emotions and groom you into sharing much more information than you feel comfortable with, so please be careful.

This being said, online ADHD communities can be incredibly helpful and a great source of community for someone with ADHD. There are thousands of people available to support each other and provide validation of feelings and experiences associated with ADHD, and often very helpful advice on these communities. It is important to recognise how much dependence you may develop on these communities, and to remember that ultimately the internet is not the real world, but to use them as a resource.

Personally, I have found one called ADHD Unlocked to be an enormous help in my day-to-day life. Not only are there regular webinars on ADHD-specific topics, but also sessions that help members focus on completing tasks that they may have been putting off and dedicated time to check in with each other. It has been incredibly helpful to find a group of people who understand my exact experiences, led by professionals who are highly experienced in ADHD.

Some communities I would recommend joining are:

- https://www.adhdunlocked.co.uk/
- https://www.facebook.com/groups/additudemag/
- https://www.reddit.com/r/ADHD/
- https://chadd.org/
- https://aadduk.org/

You may also have an ADHD support group in your local area. Check online[11] to see what already exists or consider setting up your own!

Unite: with charities

If you are interested in connecting with people who understand ADHD and potentially even volunteering to help others, it could be worth looking into the charities that are providing resources for ADHD-ers. Some of these are below:

- ❑ ADHD Foundation - 'The Neurodiversity Charity' focuses on raising awareness about the neurodiversity associated with ADHD, such as with the 'Umbrella Project 2019' which led to installations around the UK celebrating the 'superpowers' that ADHD can bring. They also have an annual conference and training courses available for professionals working with ADHD, amongst other resources.

- ❑ ADHD Action - this organisation focuses on campaigning to raise awareness about ADHD and has an impressive campaign for the UK government to create an ADHD Act which would provide additional resources and strategies for ADHD-ers.

- ❑ AADD-UK - this charity focuses on raising awareness of ADHD in adulthood, providing a considerable wealth of information and resources on their website.

You could also start your own!

---

[11] https://www.meetup.com/

Unite: other resources

There is a wealth of information online about ADHD and great books available to learn more about it in whichever area you are most interested in (in addition to this one)!

ADDitude magazine is a very valuable resource that has existed since 1998. The website is extremely comprehensive, with articles, newsletters, webinars, symptom tests and an online community.

Some excellent books that have helped me include:

- 'Driven to Distraction' by Edward M. Hallowell, M.D and John J. Ratey, M.D
- 'You Mean I'm Not Lazy, Stupid or Crazy?', by Kate Kelly
- 'Scattered Minds: The Origin and Healing of Attention Deficit Disorder', by Dr Gabor Mate
- 'The ADHD Effect on Marriage: Understand and Rebuild Your Relationship in Six Steps', by Melissa Orlov
- 'Refuse to Choose', Barbara Sher
- 'Crucial Conversations: Tools for Talking When Stakes Are High', by Kerry Patterson, Joseph Grenny, et al.
- 'The Organised Mind: Thinking Straight in the Age of Information Overload', by Daniel Levitin

is for vices

Did you know?

- ADHD has been strongly linked to problems with substance abuse such as alcohol and drug addiction. This may be because of the tendency to be impulsive, difficulties with planning ahead, and as a way of self-medicating.
- It's estimated that about 25% of adults being treated for alcohol and substance abuse have ADHD (Bhandari, 2020).
- Adults with ADHD have a higher mortality rate than those without, and are 9 times more likely to end up in prison than those of a similar age and background who do not have ADHD (Born to Be ADHD, 2017).

ADHD-ers may find that they have some bad habits as a result of their ADHD symptoms, such as impulsivity and low self-esteem. These vices tend to be 'quick fixes' of dopamine, easily accessible but with potentially life-destroying side effects. There may be a range of reasons for why ADHD-ers are susceptible to these, such as the addictive nature of the activity itself, such as drugs, or as a way of self-medicating, such as drinking alcohol to stop 'thinking'.

Such behaviour is devastating because it tends to not only be dangerous, but also worsen ADHD symptoms in the long-run. It perpetuates a cycle of impulsivity, self-sabotage and failure, leading to more bad decisions.

ADHD-ers can also find themselves seeking adrenaline or excessive stimulation to manage their symptoms, such as a restless mind. This can result in making reckless decisions and taking dangerous risks, such as speeding and committing crimes. Research has found that people with ADHD are twice as likely to commit a crime than those without it (Lanc UK, 2012). This perpetuates the negative cycle of low self-esteem and can become addictive behaviour in the chase for the 'high'. The vices associated with ADHD can also be very expensive and lead to an inability to save money or getting into debt, as in 'F is for Finance'.

Alcohol and drugs may be particularly attractive options to someone with ADHD because of the way that they 'turn off' thoughts and appear to calm us down. Addictions of these kind tend to destroy not only our own lives, but also those of the people who care about us.

Alternatively, our vices could be a little more 'socially acceptable' in the form of caffeine or sugar. These are problematic as they can go unseen by others and be written off as 'normal' behaviour. I used to quite literally live on chocolate bars and drink ten coffees a day, thinking that it had no effect on me. In reality, this kept me in a cycle of highs and lows, of being able to focus for short periods and then not being able to focus at all. The energy spikes are terrible for someone with ADHD, who is likely to already be on an energy rollercoaster. This isn't even to mention the negative effects such habits can have on our general health.

Another category of vices could be general distractions. These could include smoking (as something to do with your hands or to 'calm' you down), video games, social media, binge watching television, online shopping – anything that seems like relaxation but is actually a form of numbing yourself. These activities normally don't generally result in feeling positive afterwards, but often leave you feeling worse than you did when you entered the vortex.

The excitement that ADHD-ers may feel when they are 'hyper-focused' and doing something they enjoy can result in addictive behaviour in the form of burning themselves out. This addictive behaviour can be all-consuming and quite literally take over your life to the exclusion of everything else which is generally speaking, not a healthy pattern of focus for your brain to have. I often feel like my brain is either turned 'on' or 'off', with no in between – like a light switch. This behaviour in itself is negative because it can lead to exhaustion, as in 'B is for Burnout', and result in other negative side effects such as not eating properly or looking after yourself.

The key is finding moderation and balance. This is very difficult for me – for example I tend to be either completely vegan or a meat eater, with no in between. This comes back to setting yourself too high expectations which you are never able to meet, as in 'H is for High-functioning'.

You are a human being and it is completely normal and acceptable to live however you want to live. There is no right or wrong rule book for us to follow, but there is our own intuition about what makes us feel happy and healthy, and what makes us feel unhappy and unhealthy.

Following on from this, there are no 'set' vices other than those criminalised by law but you can use your own common sense to understand what this means for you. There are all types of addictions and things that we use to avoid our feelings, from shopping to work, alcohol to coffee, and so on. I would really recommend speaking to a qualified professional such as a therapist or doctor if you are struggling with dangerous habits, such as alcohol, gambling or drug addictions, who will be able to give you the help that you need.

Identifying bad habits

1. Make an honest assessment of your life. Write down all of the bad habits that you may have had in the past, up until any that you may have today. These could include, for example: *smoking, alcohol, caffeine, sugar, reckless driving, phone addiction, social media, video games, over-exercising, online shopping*

2. Assess each habit and how it is impacting your life. Write down all of the negative side-effects of the habit (past or present) and how much time you generally dedicate to it.

3. Now identify your 'top 3' habits from this list, and pick one that you would like to stop.

Replacing bad habits

To stop your bad habit, moderation is key. You can create a new habit to replace it by doing something consistently every day for 28 days. As everybody is motivated differently, to stop a bad habit you need to understand yourself and make your own tailored plan that you can stick to. I would generally advise against trying to stop something cold turkey, as this can easily set you up for failure. Trusting yourself to slowly change your behaviour over time is important when it comes to choosing how to live on a long-term basis.

1. Write down any ways that you have stopped doing negative things in the past, such as going to 12-step programs.

2. Identify what you are motivated by. Why do you want to stop the bad habits? Make a plan for how you can motivate yourself to want to change your behaviour.

3. Break down how you can stop the bad habit into small manageable chunks. You may find that this works best by setting yourself one goal per week, or a tiny task per day. Try to think about how you can slowly reduce the effect of the habit – for example, if you smoke, cut down on one cigarette per day for a month.

4. Ask for help. This is especially important if the habit is something that is particularly addictive or dangerous, and as above, it is advisable to speak to a qualified professional instead of trying to tackle this by yourself. Generally speaking, the people in our life should want us to be happy, and willing to help support us with changing our behaviour if we ask them. Speak to somebody that you trust and tell them about what you are doing, asking them for their help. This could involve checking in on your progress, or simply being available for a conversation when you need them, for example.

5. Identify any potential triggers or blocks to your success and prepare in advance for them. For example, this could be the situation of going out with friends which makes you want to drink alcohol or smoke. Avoid the triggers completely or as much as you can, planning for any unavoidable situations. It might be helpful to explain to people such as your friends what you are trying to do, who might suggest doing a different activity to help support you.

6. Plan to replace the vice with a positive habit. You will likely be receiving additional time and money as a result of giving up your vice so use this to be kind to yourself, such as spending the money saved each month on a yoga membership.

Remember not to beat yourself up if you do not stick to your plan. Changing your behaviour takes a tremendous amount of willpower and focus, which ADHD-ers tend to not have by the bucketload! Be kind to yourself throughout the process and simply get back on the horse if you fall off, learning from the reasons why.

is for weaknesses

Did you know?

- Research has linked 6 core themes as specific positive aspects accompanying ADHD: cognitive dynamism (divergent thinking), courage, energy, humanity, resilience and transcendence (appreciation of beauty) (Sedgwick et al, 2018).

- ADHD has been scientifically associated with having a strong sense of integrity, with feelings of being authentic and honest (Sedgwick et al, 2018).

- A 2018 study found that hardly any empirical research had been done about the positive aspects of ADHD previously. Searches for this kind of content mainly produced results about treatment - which can be beneficial, but there has been a distinct lack of research done to show the inherent benefits of having ADHD (Sedgwick et al, 2018).

This chapter is all about our weaknesses, shame and how these can actually be our strengths. By virtue of being called a 'disorder', ADHD can make us feel that there is something wrong with us - that we are weaker than others somehow. It can be easy to ruminate on this and to see ourselves as fundamentally flawed, but what is really important to remember is that your brain is just wired differently. There are literal differences in your brain to others causing your ADHD symptoms.

This isn't a bad thing, it's just different - which is actually a *good* thing. Richard Branson, Walt Disney, Zooey Deschannel and Solange Knowles have ADHD - to name but a few leading minds in our world. If we all thought exactly the same way, there would never be any new, original or creative things happening - the world would be much greyer.

Here are some of the weaknesses that we might feel we have as ADHD-ers, and how they can be turned into strengths:

- **Procrastinating and unable to finish tasks = authenticity, creativity, and learning to use our hyper-focus superpower!**

Procrastinating can be frustrating when we *really* need to get something done, objectively speaking, and literally cannot. For example, finishing a big project for work or school. We might have beaten ourselves up throughout our lives for not being able to concentrate, missing deadlines, or not doing as a good of a job as we would have liked to do.

The secret here is that you are trying to fit into a box, and you aren't meant to fit into a box. It can really help to remember that these tasks we set ourselves are ultimately small parts of our lives, and each experience helps teach us something new. As in 'O is for Organisation', we can learn how to fit into that box, if we know that it's not going to be locked shut forever. Many adults with undiagnosed ADHD may appear to be exceptionally organised in some areas of their lives, as in 'H is for High-functioning', most likely because these strategies are actually how they cope.

As human beings, we weren't designed to become domesticated, with jobs and offices and social rules and obligations. Having ADHD means that unless you actually want to do something, it will be more difficult than it would be for a neurotypical person, but the payoff is that when you find something you *do* really want to do, you can do it at a superpower level. Hyper-focus is often associated with creativity and being super-productive, and research has found that adults with ADHD had more real-time creative achievements than those without (White & Shah , 2006, 2009).

We can learn how to become organised, and how to beat procrastination. However, we don't have to give up our authenticity to do this - we can learn how to use our motivation to be super-productive at anything we put our minds to!

- **Impulsivity and changing our minds a lot = living an exciting, fun and courageous life!**

The tendency to not think things through before we do them can make ADHD-ers 'yes' people. Whilst it is definitely worth learning how to control this impulsivity muscle, seeing as there is only so much one person is capable of, it can also mean that we are very brave.

We might find ourselves in a range of exciting situations, as a result of seeking simulation, from sky-diving to writing a book, learning about our latest interest or trying out a new career. ADHD-ers tend to live memorable, full lives! Life is ultimately for living, and having a fearless, spontaneous nature can mean that we don't hold ourselves back. It's good for us to learn how to spot when it *is* a good idea to hold ourselves back, such as in 'V is for Vices', but generally speaking, there is nothing wrong with being an interested person. Curiosity has been strongly linked to ADHD - inquisitiveness, being open to experiences and having a desire to learn (Zuss M, 2012).

Changing our minds can result in a lot of shame, and problems in our relationships, as in 'L is for Love'. We might feel like we aren't able to stick at anything and feel a lot of guilt for quitting things we have committed to. However, nothing lasts forever anyway. People have a few different careers throughout their lives. In 2019, 42% of marriages ended in divorce in England and Wales (Office of National Statistics). 60% of new businesses fail in the first 3 years (The Telegraph). We can fool ourselves into thinking we need to pick one job, relationship, house and so on for our entire lives, and to do anything else is failure.

It's not - it's being human. Whilst it is very good to learn how to control our initial decisions about what we actually want to do (and how much energy or time we can put into that...), there is nothing wrong with trying things out and failing. Every failure teaches us something new, and we tend to be good at bouncing back, which is the secret to success!

- **Emotional dysregulation = extremely empathetic, energetic and likeable people!**

The differences in how ADHD-ers relate to others can sometimes cause problems, as we've seen in 'L is for Love', and 'X is for X-rated'. However, it can also result in beautiful, deep connections and incredibly empathetic people. Having ADHD can be exceptionally lonely at times, because we suffer with a lot of shame for being 'different' to others, that may have originated in childhood, when we were all supposed to fit in and achieve the same mandated level of success in our exams.

Being different can be hard, but it can also be great. I can usually tell when I meet another person who has ADHD, because they are immediately extremely warm, funny, creative and deep. They are truly interested in our conversation, instead of making small talk. They have interesting lives and are fun to talk to, even if our conversations can be a chain of us interrupting each other out of excitement!

Suffering from rejection throughout our life as a result of being different can mean that we do feel extreme pain when we sense it happening again as adults, but this also means we are capable of extreme love. We are capable of feeling things on a broad spectrum of rainbow colours, and it makes for an interesting experience of being alive. As we have typically suffered a lot of pain the past, we tend to be hyper-sensitive to others' pain, and tend to not be afraid to stand up for others when we see unfairness happening.

I believe that the majority of ADHD-ers are exceptionally kind, sensitive and compassionate. Driven by the happiness of others is not always good if it's ignoring ourselves, in 'N is for No', but as a general principle, to care about other people is something to be celebrated. ADHD has been scientifically linked to optimism, persuasiveness and an energy that energises and inspires others around them (Sedgwick et al, 2018) - great qualities to have in an employee, for example!

Though we might struggle with maintaining drama-free relationships, I like to think that we will ultimately attract people who are willing to work through any problems with us just as we would with them, because it's worth it. **You** are worth it.

- **Struggling with tasks that require sustained attention = creative, out-of-the-box and clever thinker!**

We can learn how to train our attention and motivate ourselves into doing tasks that we might struggle with, such as organising bills, even if it doesn't come naturally to us. We can ask other people to help us, or even outsource these tasks to an assistant if possible, which becomes a lot easier once we understand what we are dealing with and *why*.

If a person has undiagnosed ADHD and simply cannot do these tasks, they might be beating themselves up and too embarrassed to tell anybody about it. Understanding that our brains are simply neurologically different when it comes to our ability to do this kind of work makes it much easier to be compassionate with ourselves and ask for help, because it is not our fault.

This neurological 'deficiency' is often compensated by thinking creatively. ADHD-ers may be able to connect dots that neurotypical wouldn't think to put together, have innovative ideas and think in amazingly original ways. Richard Branson dropped out of school when he was 15, starting his own magazine and going on to become a billionaire. You aren't stupid - the system we have for measuring intelligence is. Exams and schoolwork is not the only way of being clever. Learning how to do arithmetic and chemistry equations are unlikely to help you figure out how to get a job, or do your taxes.

Learn to recognise your own intelligence and watch it grow, as in 'C is for Confidence'.

- **Overthinking and being over-energised = having a lot of excess energy to use up!**

Although it's pretty universally accepted that we need sleep, there's no reason why you shouldn't use your energy up when it is most effective. For example, if you work better later at night rather than in the mornings, who's to say you should be working in the mornings? When we know how to put boundaries in place to ensure we are meeting our own needs, as in 'Y is for Your Body', we can then work around that scaffolding to live our most brilliant lives.

Having a lot of energy means that we are able to do lots of things and make the most out of our lives. Whilst it's important that we relax and direct our energy into the *right* things for us, such as exercise or projects that we enjoy, it is a great thing that we have so much, and once we learn how to manage it most effectively, it becomes extremely valuable.

Part of understanding our ADHD is being able to manage this energy and be in control of it, so that it's sustainable. However, we shouldn't be trying to make ourselves small, feel shame about ourselves or living a life that is not within our full potential - having this much energy is an amazing thing, and inspires others around us.

- **Being sensitive to rejection and having low self-esteem: an incredibly resilient, resourceful and strong survivor!**

All lives are fraught with rejection, which if you have ADHD, can be especially difficult. Growing up with a neurodivergent brain means that you think differently to 'most' people, and simply surviving in a world that isn't designed for you is quite an achievement! Researchers have found that ADHD-ers cope well with stress, which makes us resilient - we have been able to survive despite adverse conditions (Sedgwick et al, 2018). This may be why we are excellent in a crisis, or under pressure - we are used to it!

Ironically, the impulsivity and low self-esteem that can accompany ADHD can mean we put ourselves in positions where we may be likely to fail or encounter rejection (which might be why we are always on the lookout for it)! This has definitely been the case for me, where I have had zero expectations in doing things such as publishing this book, just the hope that it might help somebody who needs it. Releasing ourselves of expectations, judgment from others and 'looking weird' (I gave up on that a long time ago!) frees us to chase our interests with a unique sense of resilience.

Although I can be sensitive to rejection from the people close to me, being bullied throughout childhood and rejected to my face more times than I can possibly count as a fashion model, means that I am pretty good at brushing off the general judgments of others. I think a lot of ADHD-ers have a similar sense of resilience in not being afraid to fail, because we are so used to failing that anything else is simply a nice surprise!

If you have ADHD, please remember that you are the furthest thing from weak. ADHD doesn't define you as a person, but it means that you are exceptionally strong for living in a world that isn't catered towards your neurodiversity. We are survivors, and living with ADHD can be incredibly difficult, especially if we don't know that we even have it. Once we understand what it is, we can then develop it to unlock the potential inside of us.

Did you know?

- People with ADHD are more likely to get divorced than those without (Orlov, 2010).

- In one survey, 42% of respondents with ADHD reported that their symptoms affected their sex lives 'a lot'. 51% of respondents without ADHD said that their partner's ADHD had a significant negative impact on intimacy in their relationship (ADDitude, 2020).

- ADHD can result in a partner shifting focus very quickly as the newness of a relationship diminishes and their attention is focused on other things. We can hyper-focus on a person, then suddenly switch our focus without intending to, causing confusion for both people in a relationship if they don't realise the changes in brain chemistry that have taken place. This doesn't mean the underlying feelings weren't real, or that they don't still exist - just possibly less intensely!

ADHD can be very difficult to navigate in romantic relationships. There are many different reasons for this, yet probably most significantly is the fact that two people are choosing to entwine their lives together, but they might think completely differently. If you have ADHD, your brain is wired in a different way to someone without ADHD - and this isn't necessarily a 'bad' thing, it's just different. However, in dating, we tend to enmesh our responsibilities, obligations and lives with another persons', and this is where the impact of having a 'different' brain can show up most clearly.

Malfunctioning 'pickers'

By pickers, I mean the tool in our brains that dictates who we are attracted to and choose to be in a relationship with. ADHD-ers are usually seeking novelty and simulation, something that will activate a production of dopamine in their minds - or someone. People who like us and simply want to spend time together don't tend to set off those adrenaline receptors, because they equate to stability, security, and a routine.

In contrast, someone who is unstable with showing affection, who might need 'saving', who is 'dangerous' and represents a challenge in some way may seem more attractive. This ties in more broadly with attachment theory[12], which relates to our backgrounds and how we received love as children. The theory says that we can have an 'insecure' attachment style, where we need constant validation and fear possible rejection, an 'avoidant' style, where we seek relationships but then avoid intimacy out of fear of rejection, or a 'secure' style, where we are happy and stable in our relationships.

Insecure and avoidants tend to date each other, because they stimulate the exact fears in each other, producing adrenaline, and the potential challenge of subconsciously rewriting your history.

If you have ADHD, you may be likely to have an insecure or avoidant attachment style. A secure style is inconsistent with the constant seeking of stimulation combined with low self-esteem and a severe reaction to possible rejection which can accompany ADHD. It can be very difficult to figure out how to

---

[12] Attached, by Amir Levine & Rachel Heller

stop being attracted to people who are simply put, not good for you.

To overcome this, it takes a lot of patience, self-compassion and self-awareness – but it can be done and is worth it. You deserve to be in a happy, loving, equal relationship.

Hyper-focused dating and disclosing your ADHD

As in 'H is for High-functioning', ADHD-ers have the ability to hyper-focus on activities, interests or people. Dating can feel almost like a level of a game to complete, because there is a sudden influx of chemicals in our brains that we don't normally have, which can literally make us feel better in terms of our general well-being as endorphins flood our brains.

'W is for Weaknesses' discussed the brilliant characteristics of an ADHD-er, which can be very attractive to someone we are dating. We might be intensely focused on the person in a way they have never experienced before, but this can almost feel like a 'high' in comparison to the 'low' that inevitably arrives as the excitement inevitably wears off. Infatuation and the 'honeymoon' period is normal to experience in all relationships, however it might feel a little more extreme for a person with ADHD, as we are capable of having such strong feelings – and acting upon them without thinking! It's important to know that the feelings are still there, just maybe not as intensely, requiring extra effort to be put in to sustain them in the long-term.

It can also feel confusing to know whether, how or when to disclose your ADHD in the context of dating. This will depend on your individual experience of ADHD and how it affects you, but in my experience it has been helpful to be open about it early on, in order to ensure that whoever I am dating is accepting of the way my brain works. Everyone will have a different understanding of ADHD and what it means, but I would say that a person who denies your experiences or thinks it is a 'problem' is someone you don't want to be with. This is in comparison to someone who may be curious and prone to possibly insensitive questions as a result of not knowing about ADHD, such as asking about medication.

Reading a book such as this one and understanding your ADHD is key to being able to communicate how it affects you in the context of a relationship, which is probably a lot more self-awareness than the majority of people have about themselves! It's also much better for you to know about your ADHD rather than be undiagnosed and unaware – so never let anybody make you feel badly about it. You also don't owe anybody the disclosure of your ADHD, if you don't want to tell them – I generally think of it more in terms of being able to work as a team with my partner.

Co-dependency

One pattern that ADHD-ers may be prone to in relationships is co-dependency. This can arise as a result of feeling 'bad' at certain things such as administrative tasks and finding a person who can either do those or provide a sense of purpose in other ways. Co-dependency is often associated with enabling addictive or negative behaviours, and involves an excessive reliance on other people for approval and a sense of identity.

This essentially means that the relationship is one-sided. Due to the low self-esteem that accompanies ADHD, we might prefer to date people who need 'saving', or looking after, so that we can feel a sense of worth in the relationship. This is perpetuating the belief that we need to 'do' things in order to be loved, and enabling negative behaviour of another person which is not a good basis for a healthy future!

It can also be a result of not understanding our own needs when we have ADHD, resulting in people-pleasing. It can feel very easy to ignore any of our own wants, needs or boundaries and prioritise the other person - especially if we are 'hyper-focused' on them!

On the other hand, the ADHD-er could be being enabled. We may be prone to having relationships where we are 'looked after', which can contribute to a parent-child dynamic - not hugely romantic or exciting! Though it can feel very reassuring in the beginning to have somebody dealing with the things that we may struggle with, such as financial matters, it is actually very dangerous to be in this position as we are vulnerable to exploitation and abusive relationships. We also don't learn how to deal with these aspects of our lives by ourselves and are dependent on somebody else - it is only when there is a problem that we might realise we have no control over important aspects of our own lives. This deprives us of responsibility and stops us being able to pro-actively manage our own symptoms of ADHD, or exist independently of anyone else.

Both of these situations can also result in resentment building up. Without realising it, we can project expectations on to the other person and think they 'should' be holding up their end of the invisible bargain of co-dependency. It's only when we sit and look at what we expect of the other person we can understand how this impacts our relationship and core understanding of love, which should be unconditional.

The resentment can feel confusing, especially for a person with ADHD who is extremely sensitive to rejection and prone to difficulties in regulating their emotions. They might react by withdrawing from the relationship and feeling excessive shame about having ADHD, which is another issue in itself - when ADHD is labelled as a 'problem' to be fixed. It simply means that you and your partner may think differently, neither of which is right nor wrong.

Arguments

The difficulties in regulating emotions and impulsivity that accompanies ADHD can result in explosive arguments. As mentioned, people thinking differently can result in different ways of living their life, and if there is not a good understanding of what ADHD involves then it can be very difficult to navigate in a relationship. The non-ADHD partner could get angry with the other person for something they simply are unable to do, continuing the shame-cycle that likely underpins many of their ADHD symptoms.

Relationships require compromise on both sides, and the ability to communicate without reacting defensively and angrily every time there is a vulnerable situation. Arguments are a normal part of any relationship, but the aspect of ADHD that can be difficult to navigate in this context is the strong emotional reactions. ADHD-ers may really struggle with understanding and regulating their own emotions and communicating calmly. It can feel as though everything is very urgent and panicked, due to our sense of 'now or never', low self-esteem and sensitivity to rejection. If arguments are not resolved properly, then they fester and build up in the background, threatening to topple everything at any time that they might be triggered.

An understanding of how ADHD can manifest is really important here, because it allows us to acknowledge the gap between thinking and acting, which can result in impulsive, hurtful choices. Both people need to be able to state their own boundaries and trust the other enough to be able to have a conversation about how they feel.

Shame

Shame is a debilitating thing to feel, and something we likely experience on a daily basis with ADHD. It can be exacerbated in the context of intimate relationships, as our lives become so closely intertwined with another's. Whereas we may deal with our ADHD in our own ways in private, suddenly having another person we want to impress potentially judge us for things we are embarrassed about, such as being messy or difficulty in handling our finances, can feel extremely embarrassing. Having ADHD itself can feel very vulnerable when talking to somebody about it who we want to accept us, especially if it's something we don't necessarily understand that well ourselves, as in 'D is for Diagnosis'.

ADHD-ers are also prone to dangerous addictions such as alcohol and drugs, as in 'V is for Vices'. The impulsivity of our brains can also result in ill-thought out decisions, such as affairs and the spontaneous ending of a relationship, which can be very painful. However, this behaviour is not exclusive to people with ADHD – people without ADHD are also prone to affairs, addictions and mistakes! If you're reading this book, then you're definitely already doing a LOT of work in understanding yourself, which the majority of neurotypical people may not be doing, and ultimately, self-awareness is what underpins this behaviour.

We all have the capability to hurt another, ADHD or not. Having ADHD simply means that you may need to be mindful about how your brain works in comparison to those of the people who you love. It is not necessarily right or wrong - we aren't in the 'hunter-gatherer' world, where ADHD would probably be very helpful in keeping us alive! We are in the world where people enter into marriages, which all have boring parts, and need a lot of sustained effort put in from both sides over a long period of time.

It is important that ADHD isn't approached as a 'problem' that one person has in a relationship. This can contribute to feeling as though you are in a parent-child dynamic and like there is something 'wrong' with the person who has ADHD, when it simply is an adjustment to figuring out what works best for both of you. As in 'W is for Weaknesses', there are also many brilliant characteristics accompanying ADHD which is what helps make us such great partners - fun, kind, empathetic, creative and thoughtful, to name a few!

Honeymoon period vs 'reality'

Relationships are hard work - for everyone! Once the happy, hormone induced high of infatuation wears off, the reality of a relationship can appear. This is when we stop projecting our hopes onto the other person of what we *want* them to be and start seeing them as they actually are. It can be a bit of a shock, as we realise that the person we thought was our soulmate actually might have different opinions to us, or might not be quite as shiny and exciting as we thought they were.

The reality of relationships, especially long-term ones, can be confronting for a person with ADHD. They involve compromise, sharing of household chores and administrative tasks, and possibly bringing up children: who are a lot of work! There's also the potential for a lot of rejection and need to regulate our emotions. It's important to be upfront and aware of how ADHD can play a part in any relationship, and to recognise any symptoms that arise as just that: symptoms. You are not your ADHD, and they can be managed in a variety of ways.

One way that symptoms could arise is distractibility. ADHD could manifest as one partner seemingly not being interested in the other anymore, especially if they were hyper focused in the beginning and became distracted by something else It can feel like our switches are either turned on or off - with no middle ground. This doesn't mean to say that an ADHD-er don't have feelings for the person anymore, but they might not be able to muster up the same intensity of passion that they had just the day before – whilst still liking their partner very much.

Other ways symptoms could arise might see the partner without ADHD becoming frustrated at their partner's inability to stick to commitments, or do household chores, for example. This can then result in a sense of 'nagging', where the symptoms are categorised as simple laziness, selfishness, or a failure to care about the other person, generally resulting in shame.

These issues can wreak havoc on intimacy. Sex can already be tough for ADHD-ers because our minds might be racing, which can prevent connection or being able to stay present. There are also practical difficulties, such as simply living by different time frames, if one partner is prone to staying up late and the other isn't. The insomnia that accompanies ADHD, as in 'S is for Sleep', can often make us feel tired and not particularly intimate!

It's important to face the issues that ADHD can cause in a serious intimate relationship head on, to communicate openly and discuss what your needs and wants are. I have found it really helpful to write down all of the ways that my ADHD could show up in a relationship, saying what warning signs might be coming up and how my partner can best help me through it. This is a really good way of clearly communicating how ADHD impacts you, as everyone has their own understanding of it, and it affects everybody differently.

<u>Tips</u>

- ❑ Be honest about your ADHD and how it affects you. Tell the other person when you feel comfortable with them and trust them!

- ❑ Try to slow down the 'dating' part. ADHD might make us rush things, and it's really important to take your time when getting to know someone, as trust is earned over time. One idea is setting a limit on how often you can see a new person in a week, and keeping a list of red / green flags. Be mindful that ADHD may make us seek out people that might not be that good for us!

- ❑ When getting into a new relationship, try to keep calm and accept the strong feelings that might arise. One way of dealing with the hormonal changes induced by infatuation could be a form of exercise, or spending more time with friends. Try not to act upon your intense feelings too quickly and acknowledge that they may be arising as a symptom of ADHD.

- ❏ Take responsibility for yourself - the only person who you can control! Therapy can be very helpful in dealing with any emotional issues that might arise in relationships.

- ❏ Don't let ADHD be treated as a 'problem', or something to be 'fixed'. It's best if both partners can accept it as a difference, which needs compassion and understanding.

- ❏ See chapter 'O is for Organisation' for advice on how to deal with chores, routines and the mundanity of life! For couples, it might be a good idea to schedule some time each week to administrative tasks. Try not to let one person take responsibility for certain areas of your life, such as finances or paying bills.

- ❏ Schedule some time each week for intimacy - such as dates, or time in bed to cuddle. This is especially important if you have different sleep patterns.

- ❏ ADHD-ers tend to crave novelty and excitement. Talk to your partner about this and how you can think of ways to keep your relationship fun, such as trying out new activities together or planning surprises.

- ❏ Make sure that each partner is taking responsibility for their own self-care and happiness. If you have ADHD, try to be mindful of ensuring that you are being as responsible as you can be for your own mental and physical well-being.

- ❏ Acknowledge and appreciate each other often - don't lose sight of what initially attracted you to your partner! A good idea is telling each other something you are grateful for to them from the day each evening before going to sleep.

- ❏ Remember to treat each other with kindness and compassion above all. Everyone will experience difficulties at some point in their life, and an important benefit of being in a relationship is the love and support that the other person can provide!

Did you know?

- There is a lot of crossover between ADHD and Sensory Processing Disorder, which can result in misdiagnosis. ADHD-ers can impact the way we experience the world through our senses, resulting in physical manifestations, such as feeling the need to be constantly moving, or excessively hot or cold.

- Research has connected problems with 'motor control' with children who have ADHD, finding that almost 50% had difficulty balancing and controlling motor function (Pera, 2015). As we don't tend to outgrow our symptoms, this can also apply to adults - making us clumsy!

- A study on adults with ADHD found that 43% of women had sensory over and/or under responsivity, compared to 22% of men, suggesting that women with ADHD are more prone to sensory issues (Brown & Dunn, 2002).

ADHD affects our entire bodies. It has been commonly linked with differences relating to how we perceive the world through our senses, with some crossover of symptoms with Sensory Processing Disorder (SPD). This disorder is not recognised as a diagnosis, but rather a description of behaviour, which is said to exist when sensory signals are not organised into 'appropriate' behavioural and physiological responses by our nervous system.

This means that we might experience the world differently to neurotypical people. I don't think there is any one 'normal' way of perceiving the world - for example, the fact that we don't all like the same foods - but it's helpful to be aware of this so that you can understand yourself, and maybe others, a little better. By understanding your own body and sensitivities, you can better understand your own needs at any one time - which is really important for ADHD-ers to know how to do. Once you can understand your needs, you can communicate them better - because if we don't understand that we are frustrated by something we can't explain that to others, and instead are prone to having emotional reactions.

These issues may also not be impacted by ADHD medication and in some circumstances could indicate the presence of other conditions, such as Autism. There are many different possible 'disorders' in relation to the senses, such as auditory processing disorder, but the key thing to bear in mind is that it is just how you are experiencing the world. There isn't any right or wrong way to experience it, and there is no one size fits all approach - even for one person, as it can change so quickly depending on our stress levels and environment.

It would have been incredibly helpful to know about this when I was a child. My parents thought that I had problems with hearing, because I seemed unable to listen and was always walking into things such as tables. Ironically, I was given fish oil, which has been proven to help with ADHD symptoms, as in 'M is for Medication', but the ADHD was completely missed until I was 25 years old.

An understanding of how sensory issues can arise in people who have ADHD can help us to spot ADHD better - it doesn't manifest physically in just one form, such as being unable to sit still. Frustration at tolerating these sensory manifestations can slowly build up in us, using up a lot of mental energy, until we 'snap' and emotionally react, possibly without even understanding where this came from. By being aware of this, we can spot any problems early on and do something to make our existence in the world a little easier!

There are typically 3 ways that we can feel sensations differently to neurotypical people. A sensory over-responsivity can result in feeling things more intensely and may provoke a quicker and more dramatic response in the body, such as gagging at certain smells. A sensory under-responsivity may arise more subtly and take a longer time to react, such as failing to notice the pain caused by walking into objects and spotting bruises on your body in the morning! The third is a sensory craving, where we may have a nearly insatiable craving for sensory experiences, such as wanting to feel intense experiences such as a very tight hug!

This is by no means an exhaustive list, but possible issues that could arise, and ideas of how to deal with them, in relation to each of our 8 senses in some way are below:

1. Touch (tactile system)

Effect	Solution
Over or under sensitivity to touch such as clothing, labels or jewellery. This could result in feeling uncomfortable and removing jewellery, for example (and losing it!).	Removing labels from clothes, wearing loose clothing or materials which makes you feel most comfortable. Laying up when getting dressed, and having dedicated places to put things such as a bowl for jewellery on your desk, to avoid losing them.

Over or under sensitivity to feeling pain	Taking precautions such as sitting in an office chair at a desk when working
Craving for intense sensations such as tight hugs.	Weighted blanket, deep tissue massages, hugs.
Dislike specific sensations such as being touched by others or certain materials.	Maintaining strong boundaries, adapting your environment to suit e.g bedsheets
Aversion to bodily sensations such as showering	Maintaining strong personal hygiene in a routine, figuring out what you like such as having baths instead of showers.
Craving constant tactile sensations such as tapping a table or scratching skin	Having a 'touch toy' such as a stress ball, or adapting your environment to suit you in a healthy way. I heard of one woman using a sandbox under her desk for her feet during the day!
Difficulty with fine motor tasks such as buttoning clothes, or tying laces.	Asking for help with tasks that cause difficulty or adapting your environment to suit, such as velcro shoes!
Tendency to be messy or not perceiving mess in the same way as others, for example not seeing dust or crumbs on a	Hiring a cleaner (!) or asking others to show you what they perceive to be clean if living with others, developing a

surface, or dressing in an uncoordinated way.	routine for cleaning, taking extra care when dressing and dedicating extra time to this.
Hypersensitivity to temperature, such as being excessively hot or cold or seeking certain states. Could also be prone to 'Seasonal Affective Disorder'.	Using a hot water bottle or hand warmers, layering clothes when getting dressed in the morning or taking additional layers with you, using techniques such as holding a frozen lemon to cool down or drinking ice-water. Using lights or goggles designed to simulate sunlight.

2. Smell (olfactory system)

Effect	Solution
Over or under sensitivity to smells such as food, which might not bother other people. This could include being bothered by certain smells or failing to distinguish between others.	Adapting your environment suitably, for example by avoiding certain smells if possible, such as going out for a walk during lunchtime in the office.
Cravings for certain smells such as strong perfume	Understanding these cravings and fulfilling them, for example by having incense, air freshener or scented candles.

| Being oblivious to smells, such as not being able to smell strong bodily odour! | Maintaining a strong person hygiene routine, showering daily. |

3. Sound (auditory system)

Effect	Solution
Over or under sensitivity to certain sounds and volumes, such as not being able to fall asleep due to a low-volume sound that others might not be able to hear such as a clock ticking.	Noise-cancelling headphones, white noise machine, regular check-ups at the doctors, ear-plugs, removing distractions from the bedroom such as clocks or switching off electronics at night.
Difficulty tolerating distractions or sounds in the form of noise, such as people speaking around you when trying to work or outside construction	Noise-cancelling headphones, asking to work in a quieter part of the room or time of day, explaining to others the difficulties that you experience in a polite way!
Difficulty listening to others and processing what is being said, such as having delays between hearing and understanding, appearing not to hear certain sounds, needing instructions repeating.	Taking extra effort to concentrate on people when they talk, writing down notes

Cravings for certain sounds such as loud music or making a lot of noise - or silence!	Noise-cancelling headphones, 'silent' musical instruments such as electronic drum kits.

4. Taste (gustatory system)

Effect	Solution
Over or under sensitivity to tastes, such as being a 'picky' eater and only liking certain types of food.	Ensuring that you have a balanced diet with enough fruit and vegetables, avoiding situations where you might have to eat food you don't like such or checking restaurant menus before dinners out. Creating a routine and planning meals.
Only eating foods at a certain temperature	Adapting your environment to this, such as taking your own food to work.
Craving for certain foods such as very bland or very spicy food, or of a certain texture	Ensuring that you have a balanced diet with regular check-ups to maintain overall health and watching out for any side-effect such as stomach issues. Consider any potential alternatives that could be healthier, such as fizzy water instead of soft drinks.

Tendency to chew inedible objects such as clothing or pens	Chewing gum, working with occupational therapists
Drooling	Working with a speech or occupational therapist, changing your sleep position

5. Visual system

Effect	Solution
Over or under sensitivity to light, possibly causing pain or difficulty sleeping	Eye-masks when sleeping, sunglasses, black out curtains, adapting environment to suit you such as having lamps or certain light bulbs.
Difficulty understanding how far an object is away from you in space, causing clumsiness or accidents	Working with an occupational therapist to develop this awareness and practice training activities, removing dangerous objects from your environment or putting stickers on things such as gates!
Difficulty reading and processing written text, for example by speed-reading but not taking in any information.	Underlining books as reading, talking about what you are reading with another person, or writing notes on it afterwards. Doing strengthening exercises such as wordsearches.

Difficulties in maintaining eye contact	Reminding yourself to look into a person's eyes when talking to them, imagining a red spot on their forehead.
Messy handwriting or a mix-up of letters or words	Working with an occupational therapist on this, practicing training activities such as word puzzles or handwriting exercises.

6. **Vestibular system: our sense of balance and spatial orientation.**

Effect	Solution
Over-responsive to movement, such as disliking playground swings or fairground rides, lifts or escalators.	Take the stairs! Explaining to others your sensitivities and adapting your environment to adjust.
Motion sickness when travelling.	Avoiding reading or screens whilst travelling, using medication, figuring out which transport works best for you.
Under-responsive to movement, such as being unable to sit still, running instead of walking, moving the body whilst sitting (such as shaking of the legs or tapping of feet).	Using distractive objects such as beads on a chain, or rubix cubes. Taking regular breaks and avoiding extra stimulants such as coffee.

Craving intense, fast experiences such as fairground rides or spinning on a chair, 'thrill-seeking'.	Engaging in safe and measured activities such as visiting a theme park (or getting a season ticket!), taking up hobbies such as rock-climbing.
Losing balance easily and being clumsy, falling over often or dropping things, difficulties in activities requiring good balance such as riding a bike.	Taking extra care when doing balance-related activities (such as using bicycle stabilisers!), adapting your environment suitably, such as having a soft carpet to fall onto, or a very tough phone case!

7. **Proprioceptive system: how we control our own body and muscles.**

Effect	Solution
Sensory seeking behaviour related to the muscles, such as excessive jumping and stomping of feet, swinging legs when sitting at a table, cracking knuckles.	Ensuring you aren't hurting yourself in these activities, avoiding extra stimulants such as caffeine, explaining your sensitives to the people around you if it is distracting to them.
Seeking 'tight' feelings such as strong hugs or many blankets at bed.	Weighted blankets, deep tissue massages, good hugs!

Misjudging how to use the muscles for certain activities such as putting arms into sleeves when getting dressed.	Figuring out how this affects you and adapting your routine to suit, for example by allocating more time to getting dressed in the morning.
Difficulty regulating pressure that is exerted, such as pressing too hard on a keyboard when typing, breaking objects or having messy handwriting.	Taking extra care when applying pressure to things and explaining your sensitivities to others or adapting your environment as appropriate, for example by using a dictaphone instead of taking notes.

8. **Interoception: how we understand our body's inner sensations, such as our internal organs.**

Effect	Solution
Over or under-responsiveness to our internal sensations, such as being able to strongly feel (or ignore!) the need to go to the bathroom.	Being compassionate to yourself and adapting your environment appropriately, such as acting as soon as you feel a 'need' in your body and knowing where the bathroom is! Try to develop a routine with 'must-do' activities each day, such as drinking water even though you might not feel thirsty or eating three meals a day.

Being aware of certain sensations others might usually not, such as the feeling of a heart beating.	Assessing how this impacts you and being compassionate to yourself - everyone has the same experiences, just some are more aware than others!
Not being able to feel pain as others might feel it, for example not realising when if you have hurt yourself and later finding bruises!	Being extra-careful to avoid hurting yourself, such as putting a layer of material on any sharp edges you might be prone to walking into.
Having trouble feeling and identifying emotions, as a result of being out of touch with bodily sensations such as tense muscles and shallow breathing. This could cause a feeling of 'numbness'.	Setting reminders to identify how you are feeling throughout the day. You might just need a few extra seconds to settle into the body and do a scan to understand how you might be feeling at any one time.
Craving introceptive input and 'feelings', such as doing things such as eating excessively fast, gripping of the hands or pinching yourself.	Trying to slow down and be mindful of how 'fast' you are living, and addressing any potentially self-harming habits. Tools such as stress balls could give a healthier effect than gripping your own hands!
Overreacting to sensory feelings such as eating more when feeling hungry.	Try to sense how you feel when you are feeling 'comfortable' by doing a scan of how all of the different

> parts of your body are feeling. Try to keep this 'normal' benchmark in mind when feeling new sensations such as hunger and eating.

It's really helpful to go through the senses above and write down how you typically experience each one. It can help make a lot of sense out of childhood habits and things we do without understanding why - try to have compassion for yourself when considering how this has impacted your life.

An important practice for ADHD-ers to do is regularly checking in to your body to understand how you're feeling - not just emotionally, but physically. I can often find myself curled up into very uncomfortable sitting positions for hours on end without realising! Think about setting a reminder to check in to your body and just sense how each part of your body is feeling, as we will discuss in 'Z is for Zen'.

Being aware of this is vital to ensuring that you are living as comfortable and happy a life as possible, and importantly, communicating this to others. As in 'L is for Love' and 'X is for X-rated', relationship issues can easily arise through miscommunications related to ADHD, and if you can't understand your own ADHD then you can't communicate this to others.

is for zen

Did you know?

- 1 in 3 people who have been diagnosed with ADHD have also experienced depression. 18.6% of adults are estimated to be affected by both ADHD and depression (CHADD, 2019).

- It has been reported that 8.3% of 585 adults with ADHD had a comorbid mood (9.3%), anxiety (8.8%), substance-use (11.5%) or behavioural (15.6%) disorder (World Health Organization World Mental Health Surveys, 2019).

- Meditation over a long period can result in different patterns in our brain, especially in the frontal region, and increase dopamine levels, which are impacted by ADHD (Zylowska, 2020).

If you've made it this far (including skim-reading or skipping chapters) — well done! This chapter is all about mindfulness and mental wellbeing. People with ADHD are highly likely to experience other mental health conditions, such as anxiety or depression, due to a range of factors including the impact of having ADHD in a 'non-ADHD' world!

Chapter 'M is for Medication' provides a good overview of treatment for ADHD, but it is a good idea to speak to your doctor about any other possible issues that you might be encountering. It's vital to accept that you are not a superhuman immune to any other mental health conditions as a result of receiving treatment for ADHD, and not to see this as a weakness. It can feel overwhelming to get to grips with one mental health condition and any more can seem simply terrifying.

Ultimately, none of us have any idea of what we are doing here. We are little bags of jelly held up by bones and our bodies are working away to keep us alive, largely without us even realising. ADHD is a label that we have apportioned to a certain set of characteristics and neurological make-up, but that doesn't mean that it is 'bad', it's just how your brain works - which is pretty brilliantly, on the whole!

Mindfulness and self-improvement can become as much as an addiction as any of our other ADHD-fuelled interests. There are certain techniques and practices, however, which can have a hugely beneficial effect on our overall mental wellbeing, which it's good to bear in mind for times of stress.

1. Meditation

This is the practice of training our attention and focus, usually associated with concentrating on breathing for a particular length of time. There are many different types of meditating, and in my experience, the sitting still for long periods of time doesn't work particularly well with ADHD. We already have trouble staying still, quiet and focused in normal life, let alone when we are left to create havoc inside our own minds with a specific goal of *not* thinking. For me, meditation is the process of training my brain to think more slowly and implement the 'thinking time' before making decisions as discussed in 'T is for Time Management'.

Meditation is the antidote to overthinking and impulsivity, by training our brains to slow down, relax and pause between thoughts. However, if we try to force ourselves to meditate in ways that don't work for us (such as sitting quietly for an hour!) we may end up beating ourselves up and quitting.

To figure out your own way of meditating, think about what makes you feel calm, and has the potential to 'turn your brain off'. Any times that you've felt completely at peace with the world, such as after a yoga class or swimming in the ocean. These tend to be activities that make us feel present and 'in the moment', such as exercising, walking or drawing, where thinking has taken a back seat to being - sometimes referred to as a 'state of flow'.

As in 'V is for Vices', ADHD-ers may be prone to developing unhealthy strategies to turn off their brains, so it's important to distinguish between 'good' and 'bad' activities. Drinking alcohol until your mind turns off isn't recommended!

When you have figured out your best fit of meditating, think about how you can incorporate this into your daily life, such as going for a run in the morning. We can sometimes need a bit of help reminding ourselves to relax, so it's good to schedule this into your routine or set yourself visual reminders.

If you prefer to try the form of meditating whilst focusing on your breath, there are really good apps such as Calm and Headspace which have a variety of engaging ways to make meditating a little bit easier.

2. Checking in with ourselves: body scans

As seen in 'Y is for Your Body', ADHD can have a huge impact on the way we experience the world around us through our senses. We might be more or less aware than neurotypical people would be of things such as background noises, lights, uncomfortable clothing, pain, temperature... the list is endless. Living in a world where we are feeling constantly stimulated can use up a *lot* of mental energy on a subconscious level, and we might not even realise that we are becoming stressed out at something - until it is too late!

It's also really useful to check in with ourselves regularly to understand how we are feeling at any one time. For example, we might have needed to go to the bathroom for an hour but ignored this need until we actually 'thought' it - or have not eaten food because we are so hyper-focused, but not realising that we are actually really hungry. Feelings are what indicate action, and they are there for an important reason! It can sometimes feel difficult to get out of my head and into my body, so these kinds of scans are really useful in connecting the two.

To do a body scan, simply think about each part of your body in turn. You might want to consciously consider the senses, such as asking yourself what you can feel, touch, smell, taste, and so on... at any one time. Or you might prefer to run through the body from your head to your feet, checking in with each part of yourself to simply 'feel' it. I find it useful to imagine that my body is a giant colouring book, and I am colouring in the parts according to how they're currently feeling - I tend to hold a LOT of tension in my body without realising! It's good to try and consciously 'relax' each part of your body.

These exercises are really useful to do a few times a day, if possible, even as mini 'mind-breaks', so consider setting yourself regular reminders to 'drop in' to your body.

3. Checking in with ourselves: feeling our feelings

It's also helpful to assess how we are feeling mentally, by asking ourselves questions such as 'how am I feeling? Am I feeling angry? Sad? Happy? Scared? Angry? Disgust?' It can sometimes be really difficult to understand how we are feeling at any one time, so this is good to do in combination with a body scan. The body sends us signals, such as tension to indicate anger, or a fast heart-beat if we're feeling scared, or the clenching of teeth if we are feeling angry.

By identifying a feeling, we can then feel it. This might be by simply sitting and allowing it to wash over us, such as with a release of crying. Or we might feel in different ways, such as writing out our feelings onto paper. It's really important that we allow our feelings to properly surface instead of trying to suppress them (even subconsciously!), to make sure that we can properly identify and act upon our needs. Feelings are what is so magic about being human - we are able to experience life in a huge variety of ways, and the negative feelings are as important to allow as the positive ones.

We are often told to just 'cheer up', 'think positively', or how lucky we are in comparison to others, as though this would fix our stresses. This usually makes us feel worse for having negative feelings at the same time as trying to get rid of them - when the only way to truly release them is by allowing them to be there. If we ignore our own needs then we end up people pleasing, as in 'N is for No', and missing out on a lot of our own life by prioritising others instead.

Try to check in with your feelings at least once a day. We can learn to regulate our feelings in this way, by accepting them instead of trying to ignore them.

4. Identifying our needs

As a combination of the two previous exercises, it is really important to regularly take the time to identify your needs when you have ADHD. If we aren't in touch with our feelings or bodies, and don't take the time to think things out slowly, we may be very prone to ignoring any of our own needs.

For example, think about your response to the question 'how are you?'. I automatically say 'I'm good thanks, how are you?' without even considering how I am actually doing. If someone asks me if I need anything, my answer tends to automatically be no - and I have to stop myself with a reminder to actually think about whether I do need something. The real answer is often very different! This relates to people pleasing, as in 'N is for No', but even with this awareness, it can be difficult to acknowledge our own needs if we have had a lifetime of ignoring them.

Our needs may vary depending on situation. We might need a change in temperature / clothing if we feel hot or cold, more sleep if we're feeling tired, to go to the bathroom, or to get some fresh air. Other needs could include taking a break from work, changing the position we are sitting in, exercise, food, drink, human connection, safety - quite literally anything at all.

Needs are typically defined as something that is necessary for our survival, and this is where we should exercise our prioritisation muscle. It can be overwhelming to think of all the things we might need in one situation, and how to distinguish them from things we simply *want*. For example, needing a glass of water versus a glass of wine!

A good rule of thumb is asking yourself: **how could I feel more comfortable in this situation right now?**

Try to identify at least one thing every time you ask yourself the question. There is always likely to be something that you can do to feel more comfortable in any situation, even if it's just taking a deep breath in.

Another way you can check in with your basic needs is to run through some basic questions as a baseline, whenever you notice yourself feeling stressed. These could include:

1. Do I feel safe?
2. When did I last drink water / eat a meal?
3. Am I hot or cold?
4. When did I last shower?
5. When did I last go outside?
6. When did I last exercise?
7. When did I last see or speak to another person?
8. How much sleep did I get last night?
9. How can I help myself right now?

Some people may find that they can identify their needs easier by writing in a journal, for example, or by speaking out loud. Whatever works best for you, make sure it's a question you're asking yourself often throughout the day - and acting upon them, communicating this to others where necessary!

5. Being aware of our inner voice and thoughts

As in 'K is for Kindness', ADHD-ers can often be quite mean to themselves, sometimes without even realising! It's really important to regularly tune in to your inner voice to see how you are treating yourself. It might seem silly to do this, but if you sit quietly for a minute then thoughts are likely to start popping up.

Notice what you are thinking about. Are you berating yourself for not doing enough, or being enough? Replaying an embarrassing scenario over in your head? Worrying about whether somebody likes you or not? Worrying about the possible worst-case scenario? Criticising yourself for your looks?

When our radio is set to 'self-compassion' mode, the above types of thoughts won't bother us so much. We might chuckle to ourselves as an embarrassing situation replays, then let it go. We consciously decide not to worry about whether someone likes us or not, because *we like us* - and it doesn't really matter, at the end of the day. We accept ourselves, and so these issues don't seem so big of a deal.

If you've only ever listened to the 'mean' radio, it's very hard to change stations - but it can be done. The idea is to catch every mean thought and turn it around, to start sticking up for yourself, to yourself. Think of yourself as calling into a radio show to complain about what you're hearing - that's inaccurate! You are perfectly great as you are! These radio presenters need firing! One of my most life-changing moments was realising that the thoughts in my head are not me, and that I can actually change them.

This can be done by taking our thoughts and asking ourselves the below questions, which have been adapted from Byron Katie[13]:

1. Is this thought true? (E.g 'X doesn't like me' - what's the proof for this?)

---

[13] https://thework.com/

2. Can I say with absolute certainty that it is true? (e.g no - I cannot say for sure, because I am not in X's head.)

3. How do I react when I believe this thought? (e.g become upset, frustrated, self-sabotage, dislike X).

4. Who would I be without the thought? (e.g calm, happy, not upset with X).

5. What's the opposite of the thought? (e.g X likes me!).

By doing this, we can see that most of what we are telling ourselves are *stories*. Choose to tell yourself the one that makes you feel best.

This applies for all of your life. ADHD can either be your favourite part of yourself, or something you try to resist. I really hope that this book has helped you realise how having ADHD is a superpower and something to be celebrated - you are something to be celebrated. Now that you have an understanding of the way your brain works; you can do anything you put your mind to.

Works Cited

Adamou, M., Arif, M., Asherson, P. et al. (2013, February 17). *Occupational issues of adults with ADHD. BMC Psychiatry 13, 59 (2013) as cited in BMC Psychiatry*. Retrieved from bmcpsychiatry.biomedcentral.com: https://bmcpsychiatry.biomedcentral.com/articles/10.1186/1471-244X-13-59

ADDitude. (2020). *Great Job! A Career Happiness Formula for Adults with ADHD*. Retrieved 12 6, 2020, from https://www.additudemag.com/best-jobs-adhd-careers/

ADDitude. (2020). *How ADHD Impacts Sex and Marriage*. Retrieved 12 6, 2020, from https://www.additudemag.com/adhd-marriage-statistics-personal-stories/#:~:text=Forty%2Dtwo%20percent%20of%20partners,intimacy%20with%20their%20significant%20other

ADHD Action. (2018). *ADHD diagnosis for adults 'can take seven years'*. BBC News.

ADHD Awareness Month . (2020). *7 facts about ADHD*. Retrieved from https://adhdawarenessmonth.org/myths-vs-facts/

ADHD Foundation. (n.d.). *Umbrella Project 2021*. Retrieved from https://www.adhdfoundation.org.uk/wp-content/uploads/2020/10/Neurodiversity-Umbrella-Project-2021-2023-Information-for-Businesses-Schools-and-Sponsors-Final-Oct-2020.pdf

American Psychological Association (APA). (2012, August 14). *Girls with ADHD at risk for self-injury, suicide attempts as young adults. ScienceDaily*. Retrieved from www.sciencedaily.com: https://www.sciencedaily.com/releases/2012/08/120814100158.htm

Attention UK. (n.d.). *University support for students with ADHD*. Retrieved 12 6, 2020, from https://attentionuk.org/about/the-state-of-current-provision/university-support-for-students-with-adhd/

Barkley. (1988). *Attention deficit hyperactive disorder-A handbook for diagnosis and treatment.*

Barkley. (2017). *Barkley: ADHD is Time Blindess.* Retrieved from https://www.youtube.com/watch?v=fVqFElTrgLw

BBC. (2020). *ADHD assessment system 'broken' with five-year waiting times.* Retrieved from https://www.bbc.co.uk/news/uk-england-53526174

Becker & Lienesch . (2018). *Nighttime media use in adolescents with ADHD: links to sleep problems and internalizing symptoms.* Retrieved from https://pubmed.ncbi.nlm.nih.gov/30223187/

Bernstein, J. (2010). *ADHD and "Honest Lies".* Retrieved from https://www.psychologytoday.com/gb/blog/liking-the-child-you-love/201002/adhd-and-honest-lies-0

Bhandari, S. (2020). Retrieved 12 6, 2020, from https://www.webmd.com/add-adhd/adhd-and-substance-abuse-is-there-a-link

Bhandari, S. (2020). *What Is Rejection Sensitive Dysphoria?* Retrieved from https://www.webmd.com/add-adhd/rejection-sensitive-dysphoria#:~:text=They%20get%20very%20upset%20if,part%20of%20living%20with%20ADHD

Biederman & Wilens et al. (2005). *A large, double-blind, randomized clinical trial of methylphenidate in the treatment of adults with attention-deficit/hyperactivity disorder.* Biol Psychiatry.

Born to Be ADHD. (2017). *A Lifetime Lost or a Lifetime Saved.* Retrieved from https://www.adhdfoundation.org.uk/wp-content/uploads/2017/11/A-Lifetime-Lost-or-a-Lifetime-Saved-report.pdf

Breslau et al. (2011). *ADHD and Long-Term Outcomes.* Retrieved 12 6, 2020, from https://chadd.org/about-adhd/long-term-outcomes/#:~:text=61%25%20more%20likely%20to%20have,36%25%20of%20the%20comparison%20group

Brown & Dunn . (2002). *Adult/Adolescent Sensory Profile: User's Manual.* San Antonio, TX: The Psychological Corporation.

CHADD. (2019, July 19). *chadd.org.* Retrieved from When Depression Co-occurs with ADHD. CHADD, ADHD Weekly: https://chadd.org/adhd-weekly/when-depression-co-occurs-with-adhd/

Cherney, K. (2019, February 19). *ADHD and Brain Structure and Function.* Retrieved November 28, 2020, from healthline.com: https://www.healthline.com/health/adhd/the-brains-structure-and-function#brain-structure-and-function

Comres. (2017). Retrieved from https://www.adhdfoundation.org.uk/wp-content/uploads/2020/10/APPG-ADHD-Jo-Platt-Oct-2020-Stakeholders-document.pdf

Conjero et al. (2019). *Association of symptoms of attention deficit-hyperactivity disorder and impulsive-aggression with severity of suicidal behavior in adult attempters.* Scientific Reports . Retrieved from https://www.nature.com/articles/s41598-019-41046-y

Cook, J., Knight, E., Hume, I. et al. (2014, March 26). *The self-esteem of adults diagnosed with attention-deficit/hyperactivity disorder (ADHD): a systematic review of the literature. ADHD Atten Def Hyp Disord 6, 249-268 (2014).* Retrieved from link.springer.com: https://link.springer.com/article/10.1007/s12402-014-0133-2

Dodson. (n.d.). *ADHD and the Epidemic of Shame.* ADDitude . Retrieved 12 6, 2020, from https://www.additudemag.com/slideshows/adhd-and-shame/

Dodson, W. (2016). *Emotional Regulation and Rejection Sensitivity*. Retrieved from https://chadd.org/wp-content/uploads/2016/10/ATTN_10_16_EmotionalRegulation.pdf

Dodson, W. (2020). ADDitude. Retrieved 12 6, 2020, from https://www.additudemag.com/adhd-sleep-disturbances-symptoms/#:~:text=Adults%20with%20ADHD%20rarely%20fall,hurts%20overall%20health%20and%20treatment

Driver and Vehicle Licensing Agency. (2020). *Psychiatric disorders: assessing fitness to drive.* Retrieved 12 6, 2020, from https://www.gov.uk/guidance/psychiatric-disorders-assessing-fitness-to-drive#pervasive-developmental-disorders-and-adhd

Holland & Riley. (2014). *ADHD Numbers: Facts, Statistics, and You.* Retrieved from https://www.addrc.org/adhd-numbers-facts-statistics-and-you/

Hupfeld, Abagis & Shah. (2019). *Living "in the zone": hyperfocus in adult ADHD.* Retrieved from https://link.springer.com/article/10.1007/s12402-018-0272-y

Karolinska Institutet . (2012). *ADHD treatment 'may reduce risk of criminal behaviour'.* New England Journal of Medicine. Retrieved 12 6, 2020, from https://www.bbc.co.uk/news/health-20414822#:~:text=They%20found%20people%20with%20ADHD,men%20and%202%25%20women

Kessler, R. C. (2005). *National Comorbidity Survey: Adolescent Supplement (NCS-A) 2001-4 as cited in National Institute of Mental Health, Mental Health Information, Statistics.* Retrieved November 28, 2020, from nimh.nih.gov: https://www.nimh.nih.gov/health/statistics/attention-deficit-hyperactivity-disorder-adhd.shtml

Kuriyan et al. (2013). *ADHD and Long-Term Outcomes.* Retrieved 12 6, 2020, from https://chadd.org/about-adhd/long-term-outcomes/#:~:text=61%25%20more%20likely%20to%20have,36%25%20of%20the%20comparison%20group

Lanc UK. (2012). *ADHD and Crime*. Retrieved from https://www.lanc.org.uk/adhd-and-crime/

LANCuk. (2016/1). *Attention Deficit Hyperactivity Disorder.* Retrieved November 28, 2020, from lanc.org.uk: https://www.lanc.org.uk/related-conditions/attention-deficit-hyperactivity-disorder/

LANCuk. (2016/2). *Our History.* Retrieved November 28, 2020, from www.lanc.org.uk: https://www.lanc.org.uk/about-us-adhd-asd-assessment/our-history

Liao, C. (2020). *ADHD Symptoms and Financial Distress.* Retrieved from https://academic.oup.com/rof/advance-article-abstract/doi/10.1093/rof/rfaa013/5824803?redirectedFrom=fulltext

M. Csikszentmihalyi & I. S. Csikszentmihalyi . (1988). *Optimal experience: Psychological studies of flow in consciousness* . Cambridge University Press. Retrieved from https://psycnet.apa.org/record/1988-98551-001

Mazzone et al. (2013). *Self-Esteem Evaluation in Children and Adolescents Suffering from ADHD.* Clin Pract Epidemiol Ment Health. Retrieved from https://www.ncbi.nlm.nih.gov/pmc/articles/PMC3715757/

Meijer, S. (2019). *ADHD can make it harder to manage your money. Here's some tips to help.* Retrieved from https://www.abc.net.au/news/2019-05-31/how-adhd-affects-your-wallet-mental-health-kids/11158952#:~:text=Adults%20with%20ADHD%20are%20far,of%20miscommunications%20in%20the%20brain

Michael Lara, MD . (2012). *The Exercise Prescription.* Retrieved from https://chadd.org/wp-content/uploads/2018/06/ATTN_06_12_Exercise.pdf

Mind. (n.d.). Retrieved from https://www.mind.org.uk/workplace/mental-health-at-work/taking-care-of-your-staff/employer-re-sources/wellness-action-plan-download/

Miranda et al . (2012). *Performance patterns in Conners' CPT among children with attention deficit hyperactivity disorder and dyslexia.* Arq Neuropsiquiatr 70(2):91–96.

Mitchell JT, McIntyre EM, English JS, et al. (2017). *A pilot trial of mindfulness meditation training for adhd in adulthood: impact on core symptoms, executive functioning, and emotion dysregulation.* J. Atten Disord.

Moya et al . (2014). *The Impact of Persisting Hyperactivity on Social Relationships.* J Atten Disord. Retrieved from https://www.ncbi.nlm.nih.gov/pmc/articles/PMC3867339/

National Collaborating Centre for Mental Health . (2009). *Attention Deficit Hyperactivity Disorder: the NICE guideline on diagnosis and management of ADHD in children, young people and adults.* The British Pyschological Society and the Royal College of Pyschiatrists .

National Institute for Health and Care Excellence. (2019). *Attention deficit hyperactivity disorder: diagnosis and management. NICE Guideline [NG87].* Retrieved 12 06, 2020, from Attention deficit hyperactivity disorder: diagnosis and management

Nigg, J. (2020). *ADHD, Anger, and Emotional Regulation.* Pyschology Today . Retrieved from https://www.psychologytoday.com/gb/blog/helping-kids-through-adhd/202008/adhd-anger-and-emotional-regulation

Office of National Statistics . (n.d.). *Divorces in England and Wales.* Retrieved from https://www.ons.gov.uk/peoplepopulationandcommunity/birthsdeathsandmarriages/divorce/bulletins/divorcesinenglandandwales/2019

Oosterloo et al . (2018). *Possible confusion between primary hypersomnia and adult attention-deficit/hyperactivity disorder.* Retrieved from https://pubmed.ncbi.nlm.nih.gov/16854470/

Orlov, M. (2010). Retrieved from https://health.usnews.com/health-news/family-health/brain-and-behavior/articles/2010/09/28/can-your-relationship-survive-adhd#:~:text=Indeed%2C%20the%20divorce%20rate%20is,The%20ADHD%20Effect%20on%20Marriage

Palmini, A. (2008). *Professionally successful adults with attention-deficit/hyperactivity disorder (ADHD): Compensation strategies and subjective effects of pharmacological treatment.* Retrieved from https://www.ncbi.nlm.nih.gov/pmc/articles/PMC5619157/

Paul Wender MD . (2020). *ADHD and Sleep Problems: This is Why You're Always So Tired .* ADDitude . Retrieved 12 6, 2020, from https://www.additudemag.com/adhd-sleep-disturbances-symptoms/

Pediatrics. (2019). *Effects of the FITKids Randomized Controlled Trial on Executive Control and Brain Function.* Retrieved from https://pediatrics.aappublications.org/content/134/4/e1063.full#sec-8

Pera, G. (2015). *Research: ADHD, Balance, and "Postural Sway".* Retrieved from https://adhdrollercoaster.org/adhd-news-and-research/research-adhd-balance-and-postural-sway/#:~:text=Was%20there%20a%20connection%20between,%E2%80%9D%E2%80%94in%20particular%2C%20balance

Perroud et al. (2016). *Personality profiles in adults with attention deficit hyperactivity disorder (ADHD).* BMC Psychiatry. Retrieved from https://bmcpsychiatry.biomedcentral.com/articles/10.1186/s12888-016-0906-6

Ptacek et al . (2019). *Clinical Implications of the Perception of Time in Attention Deficit Hyperactivity Disorder (ADHD): A Review.* Retrieved from https://www.ncbi.nlm.nih.gov/pmc/articles/PMC6556068/

Ross, E. (2016, June 16). *This is what it feels like to live with ADHD. Evening Standard.* Retrieved November 28, 2020, from www.standard.co.uk: https://www.standard.co.uk/lifestyle/this-is-what-it-feels-like-to-live-with-adhd-a3273796.html

Saline, S. (2019, August 8). *How Does an ADHD Diagnosis Affect Self-Esteem? CHADD, ADHD Weekly, August 8, 2019.* Retrieved from chadd.org: https://chadd.org/adhd-weekly/how-does-an-adhd-diagnosis-affect-self-esteem/

Sedgwick et al. (2018). *The positive aspects of attention deficit hyperactivity disorder: a qualitative investigation of successful adults with ADHD.* Springer Link. Retrieved 12 6, 2020, from https://link.springer.com/article/10.1007/s12402-018-0277-6

Stewart, K. (2013). *How Exercise Works Like A Drug for ADHD.* Retrieved from https://www.everydayhealth.com/add-adhd/can-you-exercise-away-adhd-symptoms.aspx

Takeda. (2019). *Will the doctor see me now? Investigating adult ADHD services in England.* Retrieved from https://www.adhdfoundation.org.uk/wp-content/uploads/2019/07/Takeda_Will-the-doctor-see-me-now_ADHD-Report.pdf

Taylor, S. (2018). *Examining Procrastination and Delay Among Individuals With and Without ADHD. .* Retrieved from https://www.psychologytoday.com/gb/blog/dont-delay/201809/adhd-and-procrastination

The Telegraph. (n.d.). *2019 .* Retrieved from https://www.telegraph.co.uk/politics/2019/01/24/start-ups-across-uk-going-bust-need-careful-management-economy/

University of Illinois at Urbana-Champaign. (2011). *Brief diversions vastly improve focus.* Science Daily. Retrieved from https://www.sciencedaily.com/releases/2011/02/110208131529.htm

Vanbuskirk, S. (2018, January 19). *When ADHD Is All in the Family.* Retrieved November 28, 2020, from additudemag.com: https://www.additudemag.com/is-adhd-hereditary-blog/#:~:text=Barkley.,for%20depression%20and%20personality%20traits

Weiss et McBride . (2018). *ADHD: A 24-Hour Disorder.* Retrieved from https://www.psychiatrictimes.com/view/adhd-24-hour-disorder

White & Shah . (2006, 2009). *ninhibited imaginations: creativity in adults with attention-deficit/hyperactivity disorder. Pers Individ Differ; Creative style and achievement in adults with attention-deficit/hyperactivity disorder.* Retrieved from The positive aspects of attention deficit hyperactivity disorder: a qualitative investigation of successful adults with ADHD

White & Shah . (2011). *Creative style and achievement in adults with attention-deficit/hyperactivity disorder* . Retrieved from https://addleaks.files.wordpress.com/2011/12/creativiteit_adhd2.pdf

Wiklund, Patzelt & Dimov . (2016). *Entrepreneurship and psychological disorders: How ADHD can be productively harnessed.* Journal of Business Venturing Insights . Retrieved from https://www.researchgate.net/publication/305769751_Entrepreneurship_and_psychological_disorders_How_ADHD_can_be_productively_harnessed

World Health Organization World Mental Health Surveys . (2019). *Comorbities* . ADHD Institute . Retrieved from https://adhd-institute.com/burden-of-adhd/epidemiology/comorbidities/#:~:text=An%20analysis%20of%20the%20World,or%20behavioural%20(15.6%25)%20disorder

Zuss M. (2012). *The practice of theoretical curiosity.* Springer, Brooklyn.

Zylowska, L. (2020). *Mindfulness Meditation: ADHD Symptom Relief with Breath.* (C. S. PHD, Ed.) ADDitude . Retrieved from https://www.additudemag.com/mindfulness-meditation-for-adhd/

Printed in Great Britain
by Amazon